USE
OF GROUPS
IN SCHOOLS

A Practical Manual for Everyone Who Works in Elementary and Secondary Schools

Joy Johnson

UNIVERSITY
PRESS OF
AMERICA

LANHAM • NEW YORK • LONDON

Copyright © 1977 by

University Press of America,™ Inc.

4720 Boston Way
Lanham, MD 20706

3 Henrietta Street
London WC2E 8LU England

Printed in the United States of America

ISBN (Perfect): 0-8191-0099-4
LCN: 76-50391

ACKNOWLEDGEMENTS

Many, many thanks to -

Ilene Johnson for her editing ...

Secretarial Unlimited for their typing ...

My family, Ray, Linda and Ken who helped proof-read and put up with the mess around the house ...

My parents, friends and former teachers who encouraged me to become a social worker and teacher myself ...

and

The countless teachers, administrators and other school personnel who shared their professional successes and failures with me through the years.

Note: All of the examples used throughout this book are real. The names of persons, schools and districts have been deleted or changed to protect anonymity. Many of you may feel that it is your school represented in the example. If the shoe fits ...

TABLE OF CONTENTS

FOREWORD

The centrality of school as a feature of American life and culture is rather widely recognized. The centrality of groups as a feature of school life is not so generally recognized. Nevertheless, a keen observer or participant will readily note how much of the school's instructional and facilitative work is accomplished within and through the omnipresent groups that emerge in the school, and the transactions between the school and its community.

The children and adults who learn and work in the school are involved in many groups each day. These groups, with their diverse, sometimes conflicting purposes, appear in myriad forms, and display complex dynamics. They markedly influence the individual child's ability to learn and to take full advantage of the opportunities offered by the particular educational environment. They may make or break the individual teacher's efforts to design a rich, productive learning environment and to engage the students as active, responsible participants in the learning-teaching process. Groups may enhance the school-community communications and transactions or they may disrupt or tear the social fabric of these relationships so essential to a positive learning environment and to the effective functioning of the school as a major institution of our society.

The author of this small volume is exceptionally well qualified to undertake the task she has chosen. Her thinking and writing draw upon sociopsychological knowledge and understanding of group dimensions and upon continuing analysis and evaluation of her own practice as a social worker and as a teacher. She elucidates the characteristics common to all groups. She brings shape and order among these group dimensions through specific references to groups of children and adults in the school and school-community environment, to the learning-teaching tasks and responsibilities of students and teachers, and to the collaborative efforts required for effective school and school-community functioning.

"Going to school" is a major life task of every child in our society. Groups are the major context and instruments of instruction in the schools. The groups that permeate every child's learning environment can be understood, assessed, and worked with in ways that facilitate the child's full use of growth-producing learning opportunities within the educational environment and enterprise. This small volume will be of practical assistance to teachers, social workers, administrators, parents and board members who wish to improve their abilities to understand and work with the groups that constitute the very "way of life" of the school and its community.

Mary Louise Somers, D.S.W.
Professor
School of Social Service Administration
The University of Chicago
August, 1976

PREFACE

The vast power of the numerous groups which exist within a
school is awesome. The idea for this book began when, as a
consultant for a number of different school districts, I was
witness to the energy of these forces as they operated constructively and destructively. In workshops, meetings and discussions
with people from all levels and disciplines of school systems, in a
variety of socioeconomic and ethnic communities, a consistent,
recurring theme emerged: an individual's school life is seriously
affected, one way or another, by groups within the institution. As
I consulted in one school after another, I discovered over and over
again the tremendous impact of group process upon the behavior of
members and leaders and found a multitude of ways in which a person
might intervene to effect constructive change.

The purposes of this book are to help you understand the basic
concepts of group development and functioning within a school; to
provide you with some specific interventions which you can use to
effect positive change in any group (as a member, teacher or
leader); and to aid principals, teachers, committee chairman, PTA
presidents and other assigned leaders in the administration of
their groups.

The book should prove relevant for teachers, administrators,
special educators, social workers, psychologists, counselors,
nurses, parents, pupils and others who are interested in understanding how groups function in schools.

The content is presented at a level which is geared to those of
you who are currently working within a school, are familiar with
the system, and have some self-awareness about your professional
roles and your relationship to the school. Hoepfully, you are
familiar with some of the positive and negative influences which
your school has upon the people it serves, including not only
pupils, but teachers and administrators as well. Your feelings
about the school, and your role within the system are very important. What is your own investment in being a part of your school?
What are the things you like about your job? What parts are
difficult for you to accept? What do you do to make your day in
school better for yourself? One of the main reasons why you might
want to understand how groups function in your school is because
you, whatever your position or role, are entitled to a good day.

Toward that end, the major thrust of this book is to equip you
with practical suggestions for ways to cope more effectively, have
more fun and reap more satisfying rewards within the complexity of
your school. The first three chapters are general and provide a
foundation upon which the rest of the book is built. They are
devoted to a discussion of group theory, dynamics and functioning
as they occur in schools. While the principles presented hold true
for all groups, examples illustrate how groups operate specifically
within schools. Subsequent chapters are devoted to creative

approaches to work with specific grade levels and types of school groups. Because much of the material in each chapter is translatable to other school groups, I urge you to read the book in its entirety first, and then go back to the sections which are of particular interest. Hopefully, the content is conceptually sophisticated enough for the experienced group person and straightforward and concrete enough to be of use to the novice as well.

Joy Johnson

Chapter One

THE POWER OF GROUPS IN SCHOOLS

In the classroom, gym, cafeteria, teachers' lunchroom or anywhere else you turn in an elementary or high school, group process is at work, positively or negatively affecting the functioning of anyone who comes in contact with it. The power of groups is pervasive. You cannot escape it. It is the combined power of all groups within a school which controls the school as a system. Please note that I am using "school system" in this book differently from the system meaning the collection of schools that reside in your school district. For the purposes of this book, I will use the word system to describe what happens within your school as a whole. Within your one school, what are the various dynamics that develop?

Perhaps this power is most easily recognized within the classroom -- the system that develops as the teacher or teachers attempt to impart knowledge to a number of young people with varying motivations. No classroom, however, is just a collection of individuals.

Any experienced teacher will certify that how a class works together as a group, or does not work together as a group, fundamentally affects the teacher's ability to help students learn. Even more important, at the elementary level the classroom group often remains relatively stable from year to year, with only minor changes in group membership. In these classes the primary change is the teacher, who is apt to be a different one each year.

Class Reputations

These "ongoing" groups of the same young people often develop a reputation as a group, either as a "good group" or as a "bad group". They might be "acter outers" or "good learners", or somewhere in the middle. This group reputation may keep children in a particular mold of behavior long after they, themselves, are ready to change their approach to learning.

Group reputation has two major dimensions. One is within the group of children themselves. What are the expectations members have for one another? The other is, what are the expectations held by people outside the group for group members? If you as a teacher inherit a class where the children are known to have problems, too often your expectations, your concern (or dread) about working with this particular group of young people becomes a self-fulfilling prophecy.

I recently met with a teacher who has spent much of her summer worrying about how she will maintain order in a sixth grade class she will be getting in the fall. "This class was out of control last year," she said, "and I'm afraid that's going to happen to me too because the teacher that worked with them last year was a good teacher. These are difficult children."

Now, that very well may be true, and the expectations of the class members for one another to be difficult may well continue. One thing is fairly certain, however. If she anticipates a troublesome class, she very likely will have one. The same is true for the class itself. The members' expectations and anticipations about continuing behavior, both positive and negative, will affect each individual within the classroom group. Barbara may have been a very "good" fifth grader. When she advances to sixth grade and begins some fairly typical, normal adolescent challenging not only the teacher but also her classmates may turn to her and say, "You're not like that." The peer and adult pressures may push her back toward being her old docile self. If Jim gets labeled in third grade as a "troublemaker", the students as well as his teacher may expect trouble from him, thus fostering his negative behavior long after he, himself, may be ready to try a new way of relating.

It is extremely important to understand how groups function and the kinds of pressures from within and without the group that are brought to bear on each person in a classroom. Everyone in the class - teacher and pupil alike - is affected by the group expectations. On the other hand, anyone in the class can help change what happens by acting differently.

Subgrouping

Within any classroom group are natural subgroups which develop around a variety of differing commonalities that both support and interfere with large group functioning. One fourth grade class I visited had several different subgroups, and an individual pupil might have been a member of two or three. One subgroup was boys against girls. In this class it was clear that many votes, particularly about extracurricular activities, were along sex lines. Another subgroup was the more sophisticated youngsters who tended to be rather cliquish, sticking together and looking down on others who were not socially as able as they. A third subgroup was determined by geography and by who played with whom after school. Part of your task as a teacher is to help these subgroups learn to work cooperatively together and keep from developing a restrictive cliquishness which can seriously impair learning opportunities.

Strong subgrouping in a class often creates group isolates. Two or three children may be excluded from any of the subgroups. These group isolates are frequently "different" from the other children in one or more basic ways. They may not be as bright, they may not have as much money, they may look different. Whatever the reason, these youngsters are shut out of all subgroups and frequently are the butt of negative comments from other members of the class. How to help these children become a part of the group is a task which we will be discussing in Chapters 6 and 7 when we get into the concept of inclusion of people who are outsiders.

In addition to helping natural subgroups work together, there are some subgroups that you as a teacher will want to form. These are learning subgroups established to enhance the accumulation and retention of knowledge of the students. Much group learning is stronger learning than that which is done individually. One teacher in a sixth grade class uses groups almost exclusively to teach math. She finds that by subgrouping young people, not by ability but by interest in working together, the students seem to learn better. When she gives a test, she has each student do it individually first, and then has the class go over it together in subgroups to come up with a group agreement on the correct answers. Now, that is <u>very different</u> from passing the paper across the aisle like we used to do when I was in school and grading each other's papers to make sure we were not cheating. This is a group consensus on what is the right answer, giving each individual child an opportunity to change his response if he chooses and to learn what caused him to get a different answer. This is sometimes called <u>peer support learning</u>, which we will explore further in the chapters on classroom groups.

Even outside the classroom in the school as a whole, there are strong groups of pupils that develop, or can be formed, which have impact upon everyone in the school. In one high school I visited recently, there were several specific subcultures of students: athletically oriented students, intellectuals, members of various social clubs, different ethnic groups, and "independents" who professed allegiance to no particular group. Each of these subcultures had its own way of operating, its own expectations for its members and its own relationship to the school as a whole as well as to people who were outside of that subculture.

No discussion of subgroups would be complete without mentioning administration, faculty and other staff. The faculty is, indeed, a group, with its own expectations and its own impact, and within that faculty there are frequently subgroups. Who eats together? Who hangs around together? Who confides with whom? Each subgroup has its own set of expectations for its members and its own way it wishes to relate to the faculty as a whole and to the school as a system. As in the classroom, there are frequently one or two or more teachers who are not a part of any subgroup, who are isolated and may feel real distance from other teachers. This isolation may be self-imposed or group imposed, but in either case the isolate is alone.

If there are several administrators in a school, they may form their own subgroup. Some administrators subgroup with specific teachers whom they like and trust. Unless you are a principal, it may surprise you to know that in schools where there is only one administrator often the principal finds himself isolated and alone. The other day an elementary school principal told me that he thought his job was the loneliest one he had ever had. He was expected, he felt, to give support and be available to his staff, but opportunities for him to be himself, to be real, to hurt out loud, to be acknowledged as personally important were not there. Part of my work with him was to help him find a support system for himself, to become part of some subgroup that would be important to him, that saw him as important, that would lessen his intense feelings of loneliness.

When you are thinking about the school and the groups that
exist within it, you also have to be sure to keep in mind the non-
teaching personnel — the secretarial staff (who may have their own
group or who may be part of a teachers' group), the janitorial staff
and a number of other groups within the school which are part of the
school system.   How do the various staff members in your school
relate to the students, to other staff, to each other? How does the
administration relate to the teachers and to the students?   These
questions are all part of the systems approach to understanding how
schools function.

School and Community

But you cannot limit your study of the school to what goes on
inside its walls. You must also consider your school in relation to
the outside pressures that seriously affect, positively and
negatively, how the school operates as a system.   The Board of
Education, for example, has tremendous impact upon your school's
freedom to provide creative learning opportunities for the students
and flexible teaching approaches for the teachers.   The Board of
Education is also a group, and how its members function together
and their expectations of one another, and of you, seriously affect
the kind of teaching or helping you will be permitted to do.

The community as a whole also has certain expectations for the
schools within it.   In one school, residents of the surrounding
community were so concerned about the amount of noise that the
young people were making during recess that they put immense
pressure upon the principal to have only indoor recess, and he gave
in to their demands. The only way to manage this, because of the
space problem, was to have each teacher conduct her own recess with
her own children in her own room. This outside community pressure
thus had tremendous impact upon the teachers' ability to teach
because recess time had been "refueling" time for the teachers in
that school.   They had used that time to relax, rap with other
teachers, plan what to do next in classroom activities, and for
many other personally satisfying experiences which could be crammed
into that twenty minutes.   Having this time snatched away due to
community pressure was detrimental to everyone in that system.

Another powerful outside source of pressure is the parents of
the children whom you serve.   Individually and collectively,
parents are of real importance to the school, with a great deal of
influence which will help or hinder the educational process. Most
parents are also part of one or more community subcultures, each
with its own expectations for children and the school. If academic
achievement is highly prized by one group, a parent who might
otherwise accept her child's difficulty mastering spelling, might,
as a member of that subculture, put enormous pressure upon her son
or daughter and the teacher to achieve beyond the child's current
ability.   The need to compete in accordance with the expectations
of other members of that community subgroup may take precedence
over concern for the child, at least temporarily.

Groups of parents may socialize together, or may form a group for some purpose related to the school. How they function as a group influences greatly their approach. Some parents band together in anger, attacking the school and putting personnel on the defensive. Others are more constructive in their approaches. There will also be times when, in addition to responding to natural parent groups, school personnel may choose to form parents groups for a variety of reasons which will be discussed in Chapter 14.

There are, of course, many other outside organizations and groups that affect the inside system. I will touch upon these occasionally as I wend my way through the study of group process, how it works, and how to influence it. It is clear that many outside organizations approach or respond to the school to meet their own needs.

Group Decision-Making

In the years that I have been working in schools as a teacher, a school social worker and a consultant, I have learned never to underestimate how strong group pressure is. What is happening among group members seriously affects the basic decisions made by that group. At a recent elementary school faculty meeting, a decision was made based on members' feelings about one another, rather than on an objective look at the issues. The problem under discussion was merely a vehicle by which faculty could express their anger at each other. This particular meeting was called to decide whether children should be allowed to play in the gymnasium when they were finished eating lunch. In the past, as soon as children were through eating, they were herded outside to "let off steam", with problems occurring because of lack of adequate supervision. The lunchroom supervisor, who was also a teacher, suggested that manageable numbers of these children be allowed to play in the gym, using activities which he would like to organize and run.

This particular lunchroom supervisor was part of a small subgroup of teachers who had decided, for a variety of reasons, not to join the school's teacher organization. Many of the other teachers were very angry at this subgroup because of that decision. As a result, the discussion about the children was distorted by that dynamic, rather than focused on what was indicated for the young people. The other teachers were so angry that it was difficult for them to hear what the supervisor was saying about his plan, and their anger at him was acted out in a punishing way toward the very children they cared so much about. I wish I could say that this was unusual, or a unique situation. However, I am sure that as you think about it you will find ways that your school operates based more on how people feel about one another and how the groups function together - or do not function together - than on the feasibility of the decision being made.

Groups, then, have the power to make decisions which are counter-productive because of the destructive ways in which they are functioning. But groups can also be very powerful in a positive way too, and an important part of the task in this book is to examine ways that the power of groups can be harnessed for positive effects. In one class where there were two or three young people who were not learning satisfactorily, a teacher used the power of the classroom group to motivate these children to buckle down thus creating a growth in learning. There were many vehicles she used to do this, some of which will be covered in Chapter 7. But there is no question that this class was a powerful influence on some non-learners in a very constructive way.

Your Power in Groups

A school is a system where every individual who walks in the door ought to feel valued as a worthwhile human being. Too often, instead, people (students and faculty alike) feel like they are an insignificant member of a huge bureaucracy. The groups of which you are a part contribute greatly to these positive and negative feelings. Your understanding of the dynamics and meaning of the things that happen in these groups is a key to making your life in school more satisfying.

Think about your school for a moment, if you will. Think of the number of groups that you are a part of, the number of different subgroups that you belong to, and think selfishly, just for a moment, about what it does to you to be a part of these groups. Are there some groups in which you feel significant and valued? Are there others in which you feel frustrated and angry most of the time? If you are a teacher, when you close the door to your classroom do you feel that the young people are expectant and excited about learning with you? Or, do you feel hostility as you close the door, both from you and from them? When you sit down in the faculty lunchroom, do you always sit with the same group of people? Do they make you feel valued and cared about? Are they people whom you trust? Can you risk with them? Can you tell them where you "blew it" and still feel okay about yourself?

Now take a step back, for a moment, and look at your school as a whole. Which are the groups that you think are functioning well? Which are the ones that are having difficulty? What is it like to be in a faculty meeting in your school? A committee meeting? A curriculum planning meeting? A pupil personnel staffing? How are these groups functioning? What would you change if you could?

As you become more tuned into group dynamics, you will dis-cover your power to help facilitate better group interaction. Every member of a group affects what is going on whether he knows it or not. If you choose, you can play a conscious part in helping any group you are in to function in a more productive and satisfying way. You may also choose, as often as you like, to stay out of the group process and not try to help it function better. You may decide to protect yourself and avoid the pain of trying to interact. Or, perhaps you do not know what would be most helpful. Whatever the reason, you have a _choice_ once you understand what is happening within a group.

Most of you will find some times when you _wish_ to be helpful but cannot, and others when you choose not to try. There are times,

however, when your helpful attempts do not succeed, perhaps because
you are not in tune with the group. Personally, I have the most
difficulty responding to group process when I have such an
investment in the outcome that I get far ahead of the other group
members and lose touch with their priorities. Now, there will be
times when you may want to take over, become a strong leader, get
ahead, and pull like mad toward a certain goal. If, for instance,
you have a curriculum report that has to be finished by Friday,
there is no time to sit back and ask the group members how they feel
about writing a section. That is the time to come on strong, to
pull them into task completion, to rally them around you and to use
the way the group functions to complete that job. Other times when
you might want to exert controlling leadership might be in
organizing, in getting a difficult task completed, or anytime that
getting the job done becomes more important than keeping the group
functioning well together. In taking a strong leadership stance,
you will need to know group dynamics, but your function in that type
of group is very different.

In another kind of group where you are a leader, you may want
to facilitate group process rather than pull toward a specific
goal. For instance, there was a faculty meeting I attended not long
ago where the faculty had split down the middle trying to decide an
issue about grading. Half of the faculty was in favor of much
stricter rules for grading, and the other half was really resistant
to tightening up the rules. The principal was able to ask if they
could agree on something in the middle, to satisfy both sides. If
he had had a tremendous investment in one side or the other, he
could not have done that. Because he was able to relate to the
process of what was going on and did not have a strong personal
interest in the outcome, he was able to facilitate reaching some
kind of mutually agreeable consensus. Now, he might have chosen
not to do that. He might have sat back and watched them fight, or
he might have made an arbitrary decision himself. Because he
understood what was happening, he was able to make that a conscious
choice. Later in this book we will discuss the various dynamics of
polarization in groups and what it is that causes groups to
dichotomize.

Interventions in group process can be constructive, facilitative and helpful. They can also get in the way of group progress
and be destructive. If you are a teacher trying to hold a classroom
meeting, and one pupil or several pupils do all the talking, you may
feel that you want to intervene. Your intervention can facilitate
the process or it might make things worse. A third grade class was
holding a classroom meeting and two boys talked and talked and
talked until the teacher could not stand it anymore. She turned to
them angrily and said, "If you two don't shut up, I'm going to send
you out of the room!". She did shut the two boys up, but she also
gave a message to all the children in the class that maybe it was
not okay to talk. She had spent three days telling the children
they could talk during this twenty-minute classroom meeting, but
after this intervention, many in the class felt she did not really
mean it. Her verbal attack set the group process back quite a bit.

There are many other ways that she might have been able to handle this monopolizing which would have been constructive and supportive to the group process rather than getting in the way. She might have ignored the talkers and asked the other group members to talk more. Or, she might have assigned the two talkers the job of helping the other, less verbal, children talk up more thus channeling the need for attention. As she and I talked about it later, we thought of additional interventions which might have been helpful. She then had a chance to go back, to function differently and to recoup her losses.

Always Another Chance

One of the things that is great about groups is their tremendous resiliency. While everyone that is a part of a group can have some impact on what happens, no one individual is so powerful that he or she can make drastic changes without the cooperation of the group itself. The task in the remaining chapters of this book will be to spell out why that is so, to help you learn how to observe what is happening in the group process, to understand it and find ways in which you, being who you are, can make conscious choices about where and when you want to intervene.

Chapter Two

WHAT HAPPENS IN ALL GROUPS

While each of us participates in many groups in a variety of settings each day, we often do not pay attention to how the group in which we are currently functioning operates and what we do that helps or impedes that process. A number of readers may be asking, "What do you mean by process?" The term "process" has a highly specialized meaning in a number of different fields. In interactional theories, "process" usually refers to the ongoing nature of interpersonal relationships in all their dimensions. Group process in any one group within a school setting might well include anything interactional that happens within that group - among the members and between the members and the teacher or leader. This process affects the way each group is operating internally and with other school groups. This rather global definition may become clearer as I point out some of the various components of group process which operate continuously in schools.

Levels of Interaction

In addition to group process, there are two other levels of group interaction. Every group operates simultaneously at three levels, and it is often difficult, if not impossible, to separate out the group process from the other two levels of interaction. The most obvious is the content or task level. What is the group discussing or trying to achieve? As a principal opens a faculty meeting or as a teacher begins her lesson, both have certain content which they wish to cover. Content is a significant part of what is happening in any group at any given time. As you become aware of other levels of interaction it is important not to lose sight of the content or task.

Another level at which a group is always operating is the personal level. That level is where each person brings his own individuality into the group setting. Each person in the group has his own goals, his own expectations, his own ways of relating and his own feelings about himself. All of these affect the group process as well as the way the group undertakes the task or masters the content presented. It is important for every group leader to respect and understand as much as possible about each person in the group. The leader will want to know each person's priorities, his individual needs and the kind of relationship he is seeking with other members and with the leader.

Content, process and personal. All are levels of interaction in groups, each affecting and being affected by the other. Each of them is significant, though at some points one may be more important than the other. When you have a deadline, for instance, task completion must take precedence over the other two levels. If

you are working in a therapeutic group of children, and one member
is facing a crisis, the _personal_ level is temporarily the most
significant. When group members are having difficulty relating to
each other, the _process_ level looms largest.

Once when I was explaining this concept to a group of
teachers, one of them loudly complained, "Good heavens! It's
difficult enough for me to keep my mind on what I'm trying to teach,
and now you're telling me I have to watch two other levels at the
same time!" I certainly can understand how that teacher felt, and I
agree that watching for all three levels is more complicated. I
would also agree that it is unrealistic to expect yourself always
to be able to tune in at each of the three levels of group
interaction. On the other hand, if you can keep in tune with these
levels most of the time, your perspective and freedom to intervene
will be much broader. Your awareness that the group is functioning
at each of these levels frees you as a teacher, administrator or
facilitator to move in at any level when an intervention is
indicated.

Recognizing Level Priorities. In a classroom a teacher may
choose to put aside the content because some person in the class is
deeply hurt, and for a time the student's need takes priority over
mastery of the day's lesson. I walked into a junior high class one
day and found a whole group of subdued young people discussing with
a girl the upcoming divorce of her parents and her bind in having to
choose with whom she would live. This was not a therapy session for
the girl, but everyone in the class empathized with her pain and
gave her support. The teacher, I believe rightly, had decided that
for that half hour helping this girl was more important than
spelling.

When I have mentioned this possibility to teachers some have
said, "I agree, but I am afraid that if I let personal problems take
over, the entire day will be spent on these issues and nobody will
ever learn anything. The kids will take advantage of it. They'll
keep thinking up problems just so they can talk about them." I
think there is some risk that this could happen, but it very rarely
does. If young people know that personal time is very precious and
is to be saved for extremely important issues, they tend to stay
within those bounds. If it begins to be abused, however, there are
several possibilities for changing the focus. One teacher, when
she felt personal discussions were getting out of hand, said,
"Okay, we also have work to do. Let's set aside the last hour of
every Friday for rap time when all of you can talk about anything
that's important to you." She had students submit requests for
items for the agenda which were acknowledged at the beginning of
rap time. Sometimes rap time was used for a confrontation with the
teacher about something that had happened during the week, such as,
"How come you gave us three tests this week when you promised to
give us two?" This teacher found this method helpful as a means of
knowing her students' gripes. Sometimes a class member wanted to
discuss personal problems. Other times there were broader school
issues that the students wanted to address. Whatever it was, this
time was set aside for things that were important to the students.

It is interesting that every kindergarten I have ever visited has a "show-and-tell" time where children can talk about things that are important to them and bring things from home to show off. Yet, somehow, when you reach third grade such sharing of yourself becomes no longer acceptable in most schools. Perhaps it is time to build that caring into upper grade levels so that the personal level of group interaction will again be valued in the classroom.

There will be times, too, when the process level takes priority, when the children are relating in a way that obstructs learning. Perhaps they are so angry with each other, provoking each other so much, that they cannot learn. At these times the teacher may wisely make a decision to put aside the learning task for that day and to talk about, "How can we work more cooperatively together?"

Possible Level Interventions. How many of you have ever looked at your faculty, class or therapeutic group and suddenly got the feeling that everyone in that group, perhaps including you, would rather be somewhere else? It happened to me one bright, sunny day when I was giving a lecture to graduate students on the history of adolescent development. I suddenly became aware of a group of bored, polite students, none of whom seemed the least interested in what I was trying to say.

After dealing with this blow to my ego, I was able to think about those three levels of interaction and make a choice at which level I wanted to intervene. I could have changed the content, since it was obvious that my lecture on the history of adolescent development did not particularly intrigue nor excite my listeners. I could have chosen to change the subject, tell a joke or do something else to regain their attention at the content level. But I also had other choices. There were many interventions I could have made at the personal or process level. I could have looked at the group and smiled, saying, "Hey, it looks like everybody here would rather be somewhere else. Where would you rather be? What's your thought about being together and listening to me?" That process intervention might very well have gotten us into a good discussion of what had happened in the class and how we could work better together in the future.

Or, I could have decided to intervene at the personal level. Each teacher or principal has somebody in the class or on the faculty that they consider an ally, whom they can count on to come through when things get rough. They also often have one or two people who act as adversaries, whose purpose seems to be to make it difficult for the leader or teacher. Had I decided to intervene at the personal level, I might have turned to one of my allies and said, "Bob, what do you think about what I've been saying? Is it relevant for you?", in the hope that he was tuned in enough to me to give an honest response that was not attacking. Or, because I was upset that no one was listening, I might have turned to one of my adversaries and said, "Barbara, why aren't you listening?" That would have gotten the group's attention, but with possible strong, negative side effects.

Since a teacher or group leader has more than one alternative at each of the three levels, she will quickly develop a repertoire of possible interventions which usually work for her. Hopefully, you will feel free to exchange ideas with your colleagues about interventions which have worked. What type of interventions do you use to help the group take hold of a task when things begin to go awry? How do they work?

As you think about this, you may find that most of your interventions take place at only one of the three levels, rather than being distributed among personal, process and content. If that is the case, and it is with most people, you may want to think about the possibility of increasing your options by considering the other two levels. One therapist with whom I consult began most of her interventions at the personal level. Anytime the group slowed down or floundered she would reach out to one member with an interpretation or question. As she began to think more seriously about the other two levels she saw that she was inhibiting the potential of the group by sticking to the one-to-one. She saw dramatic results as she began to aim some of her interventions at the issue or content being discussed or at the group process level.

The next time you are in a group meeting where your own role is inactive enough so that you can pull back a bit and watch what is going on, keep an eye on these three levels of interaction, content, process and personal, and see if you can observe what is happening at each level. You may want to go a step further and decide, if you were the leader of that group where would you intervene? At which level would you want to make an impact? What would be some possible interventions you could make at each of the three levels?

Stages of Group Development

In addition to the three levels at which any group interacts at any one time, each group goes through different stages of development, which also affect the group process and how the group functions.* When a class begins in September or when a therapeutic group has its first and second meeting, group members are trying to decide whether they want to be a part of that group at all. Even if children are assigned to a group, or you are part of a faculty by administrative directive, you still decide if you want to belong to that group. Are you going to like it in that group? This yes or no question is decided in the first stage of group development. It is here that each individual makes an initial decision about his membership in the group. In addition, groups as a system make a decision about whether or not they want to exist. A committee or therapeutic group meeting for the first time may, for a variety of reasons, just not get off the ground. Members may feel there is

---

*For a complete discussion of these stages as they relate to socialization and treatment groups see Bernstein, Saul, Ed. Explorations in Group Work, Boston: Boston University School of Social Work, 1965.

little hope for the group and decide to disband. Other groups may dissolve without ever discussing the decision to do so.

The beginning stage, as with the other stages, combines both the individual choice and the group choice regarding the viability of the group. This group decision may be a subtle one. Too often social workers in a school have formed therapeutic groups without relating the goals of the group to those of the members. The members may agree to come, but never want to belong. This usually results in a pattern of spotty attendance, with the social worker trying desperately to get a full group together. This "hit or miss" may go on all year or the worker may give up and cancel the group. There are many reasons why this attendance problem might occur, but one of the most frequent is faulty resolution of the first stage of development.

If the group has agreed to exist and each person has made his choice about remaining an interested member, it then moves (roughly or smoothly) into a second stage in which the group determines how it is going to operate. In this stage each member works on finding a place for himself within the group, and the group as a whole determines the group rules, expectations of one another, how the group decisions are going to be made and whether the group goal is a manageable one. This stage sometimes moves smoothly, but more often than not there is a stormy period as members jockey for position, test the teacher or leader and try to find mutually acceptable ground rules.

If that stage is successfully completed the group usually goes into a phase of being very close to one another, very cohesive and develops a strong feeling of class or group unity. During this stage members often form an identity with the teacher or leader. This is not, however, a stage of great task accomplishment. During this phase the feeling of being together is so good, feels so nice, that group members frequently hesitate to do anything that might "rock the boat". They do not want to challenge each other, question each other or be too open with each other for fear that in doing so, good feelings will be destroyed.

It may be a relief, then, when the group moves into the next stage of development, where people feel safe enough with each other and comfortable enough with the group as a whole that they can risk being more open and direct. In this stage the group is solid enough that group members dare question and challenge one another and set limits, as well as offer a great deal of support. In this stage the trust of one another and the leader, teacher or principal has usually developed to the point that challenging is a natural phenomenon. For all of these reasons it is in this stage where most of the content or task is mastered.

The last stage, the ending stage, occurs when the group is close to termination. It might be the end of the the school year, the end of the contract of a therapeutic group or a completed task. Regardless of why the group is ending, members need time to cope successfully with the fact that they are leaving each other and the group.

Components of Group Process

Not only does a group operate at three levels and go through
five stages of development, but also there are several components
of group process which are important to keep in mind. Most of these
components are initially resolved during the second stage of
development when the issues of how members are going to work
together are thought out, fought out, spelled out and resolved.
While these elements of group process are not rigid, once they are
established, they are very difficult to change. Many teachers and
leaders of groups in a school are very active at the process level
during that second stage of development to try and help the group
establish ways of functioning which will be supportive to the
reason that the group exists. (See Chapters 3 and 6)

Norms. When I see a group operating one of the first things
that I wonder is, what are the group norms? There are many different definitions for group norm. The one that seems most usable
for groups in a school setting defines a group norm as an expectation for behavior which the members of the group agree should
exist, whether or not they follow it. The key word here is "agree".
An individual member or leader may expect or desire a certain
behavior, but if the other group members do not agree, it is not a
norm. A teacher may feel swearing is inappropriate, but if her
students do not agree that she is right, her expectation is not a
norm though it may become a rule that the students are expected to
follow.

Every teacher, facilitator or leader has certain rules about
group behavior: "You can't hit anyone in the group - I don't want
anyone to get hurt." Or, "You can't steal something that belongs to
someone else." These rules are imposed by the leader for whatever
reason he or she decides. Or, rules may be made by group members
themselves. Rules are enforced outside the group, while norm
enforcement is internal. Rules may or may not become group norms,
for a group norm is something which is worked out and resolved by
the group itself. Consider the "No hitting" rule, for instance.
The teacher may say to the class, "People can't hit each other in
this class, and if they do, they will be punished." If the children
agree that should be a rule, then the likelihood is that they will
make it a norm and enforce it among themselves and the teacher will
have little punishing to do. If, however, the children do not agree
that it is important, if they never accept it as a group norm, then
the teacher may spend a year trying to enforce that rule.

Another side of the same coin is that the children may establish group norms with which the teacher does not agree and finds
himself fighting against. In one classroom the children decided
that they could do whatever they wanted to as long as they did not
get caught. It became a norm to see what they could get away with.
Without ever discussing it the students developed a "Let's see how
much we can get away with" norm, and during the entire year, there
was a great deal of subtle acting out which made it extremely
unpleasant for both the class and the teacher.

It is easy to see that norms can be either constructive or destructive. It is important, then, for the leader of any group, whether it is the teacher in the classroom or the facilitator in a treatment group, to help that group develop constructive group norms, since once they are established they are very difficult to change. A faculty at the beginning of the year develops norms which both enhance and inhibit their functioning together. One faculty had a very strong norm that everybody was supposed to do as much work as they possibly could and that a good teacher was one who came early, stayed late and worked very hard. I knew that it was the norm in that school because a teacher who was leaving at 4:00 (the official ending time was 3:30) apologized as she left, saying, "I'm taking work home, and I have a dentist appointment."

If it had not been a group norm that people were supposed to stay late and work hard, she would not have felt a need to apologize or explain why she was leaving at 4:00. Some of you may see that as a constructive norm and others as a destructive one, but however you evaluate it that norm certainly had a lot of power over the teachers in that school.

Another school had what I considered a very destructive norm, "You can say anything you want about someone as long as you don't say it to the person's face." In that particular school most of the confrontation, most of the criticism and most of the support was underground. If you were across the hall from me and you did something which I did not like, I probably would not tell you about it. Instead, I would gossip about it to someone else in the teachers' lounge, and you might never know why I was angry or even that I was upset at all.

Children, too, may develop destructive group norms. In one junior high school a norm was established not to talk with members of a different subculture. This made it extremely difficult for the student council to operate or for class members to complete group projects together.

Take a look at the norms that are operating in your school. What are some that are working well, that seem to enhance the way the group operates together? What are some that get in the way?

Roles. Each group, large or small, has certain functions that are assigned to individual members. These functions, or roles, significantly affect the group as a whole. It is interesting to note that in spite of the frequency with which roles are referred to in the group literature there is no agreed upon definition. There is some concensus, however, that a role is a set of expectations for a person occupying a position within a given system. Role assignment is a two-way process. For any person to be in a role it takes both the willingness of the group for that role to be held by that person and the person's willingness, conscious or unconscious, to accept that role.

There are two types of roles. Some roles are necessary for the functioning of any group. These I call basic maintenance roles.

Others, negative roles, are dysfunctional to group operation and are symptomatic of malfunctioning within the group. There are four basic maintenance roles which must be filled for any group to function in a positive manner. Frequently, these basic maintenance roles are flexible and in any class or group you may have two or three people who can play each of the roles. Even if a role is usually fulfilled by one person, others may move in and take over if that person is absent or is temporarily not able to function. Many people are able to play different roles at different times, depending on their interests and the needs of the group. This role exchange is frequently seen in well functioning groups. The more flexible the basic maintenance roles are the healthier the group. These basic maintenance roles are necessary for any well functioning group, whether it is a faculty, class or treatment group.

To begin with, each group needs somebody indigenous to become a leader. Even though a teacher may be in charge of her class, there is always somebody within the group who leads the other children, one way or another, and that is a very important function for the group. The indigenous leader might be the person in the class who decides what to do if the teacher is late for school or who calms the other children down when they get out of control, or when the class is resisting decides, "Oh, let's give it a try." The leader, of course, can also be destructive in the way she functions in the class. She may encourage the class to refuse to cooperate with the teacher or ridicule children when they try to participate. But whether she is constructive or destructive, she fulfills an important role in the class.

The same is true in faculty groups. There are usually one or more leaders who operate either cooperatively with the administration or in fights against it, who are expected to represent some of the faculty's views and lead the group. Now, in some classes and in many faculties each subgroup that I discussed in Chapter 1 has its own leader, and how these various leaders work together (or do not work together) greatly affects the functioning of the group. But certainly, every group in order to operate in a constructive way needs to have somebody, or a collection of people, to whom they can turn for leadership.

Another needed role is the group nurturer. The group nurturer is the person who cares for people, who sees that their needs are taken care of, who puts on an emotional bandaid if someone gets hurt and who does a great deal of "giving". The group nurturer might be the teacher who brings cupcakes to the faculty meeting or the young person in the classroom who comforts or hands kleenex to the child who is crying because he feels picked on by the other children. The group nurturer can be someone of either sex and is usually somebody who is fairly widely accepted. Nurturing is very important within the group setting and each group leader or therapist needs to help this quality evolve in every group.

Another basic maintenance role is that of enabler. The enabler is the person who sees that everybody's point of view is

taken into account. Without necessarily "taking care" of a person
as a nurturer would, the enabler feels that each group member is
significant and deserves to be heard. It is the enabler who says,
"Hey, Teacher, Johnny didn't get to finish what he was trying to
say," or who reaches out to someone to be heard in a small group
discussion. It is the enabler on your faculty who tries to include
others in the decision-making process, and who gets the group to
slow down so that it does not run over people. As with the other
roles, the enabling function is very important for positive group
interaction.

A role which I have found to be basically important in helping
groups operate, but which may surprise you, is the role of subject
changer. A subject changer is someone who is in tune with the pulse
of the group and who somehow knows when the topic under discussion
is either too heated, too boring or irrelevant to the current
group. At such times he moves in to help change the subject in a
variety of ways. Examples I can think of are the youngster who
knocks over his chair every time the lesson gets too hard, the class
clown who cracks a joke when people begin to argue or the teacher
who brings up a new topic when an impasse develops. You may feel
these are destructive actions and in some cases that may be true.
However, I have found that groups do need someone to change the
subject, whether they be faculty groups, therapeutic groups or
classroom groups. Because groups are such powerful forces in
schools with so many differing functions, it is easy for the
process to become overwhelming. The conversation may be too
argumentative to be safe, too confusing to be understood or too
boring to keep one's attention. In any of these instances, a
subject changer plays an important role which fulfills a need for
the group even though it is distressing for the leader. Helping
that role evolve may let the subject changer function in ways that
are less frustrating to you and more constructive to the group.

I am sure you can think of many other basic maintenance roles
that are being fulfilled in the groups with which you have contact,
but the ones described here are the core, the very essence, in my
experience. Unless these roles are fulfilled it is very difficult
for the group to function in a constructive way, and the
fulfillment of these roles, as I mentioned before, requires both
the willingness of the person to play that role and the willingness
of the group to let him do so.

There are also roles that are negative that I consider sym-
bolic of a problem in the group process. Since the behavior of a
member in a group is conditioned not only by his needs and
willingness to behave in that way but also by the group's collusion
or willingness to let him do so, even the negative roles reflect the
dynamics of what is happening in the group. In following chapters
are examples of how negative roles operate in a variety of group
settings. For now, it is important to take a general look at what
these roles are.

Perhaps the most obvious is the role of scapegoat. Scapegoating occurs in two ways, either simultaneously or one way at a

time. One way of being scapegoated by a group is to be set up to
act out for the group. If I come on too strong as a teacher, and
the students question whether it is going to be safe to challenge
me, one person in the group may attack what I say, thus acting out
for the rest of the group. In a classroom where most of the
children are very well behaved, frequently there are one or two
youngsters who act out a great deal. They are acting out for
themselves and because they need to act out but also because there
is something in the rest of the class that says, "Hey, we need
somebody to act out for us." The class may pick on that person and
complain about her behavior even if the perpetrator is acting out
for them.

I was demonstrating a classroom meeting with a fourth grade
class when one young man began to fight, push and punch other
children. After many unsuccessful attempts to help him control his
behavior, I finally asked him if he wanted me to ask him to leave
the group, if that was his goal. He looked smug and said, "Yes."
With that response I abruptly changed the topic of discussion to,
"What happens if you behave in a way that the teacher asks you to
leave?" Instead of bawling him out I decided to ask each person in
that group what it would mean to him or her to be asked to leave.
The result surprised me, despite my years as a teacher, because
many of the "good" children said that they had always envied those
children who had the nerve to behave badly enough to get sent out.
As we discussed this it became evident to me that what this young
boy was doing was not only for himself but for the vicarious
satisfaction that some of the "good" members of the class gained
from his misbehavior. While they got mad at him for disrupting, and
their anger was real, there was also a piece of them that enjoyed
what he was doing, whether they admitted it or not.

Another form of scapegoating occurs when a child, usually one
who is different, gets picked on by the other children. That child
might not be quite as bright, be a different color or wear unusual
clothes. To create this form of scapegoat also requires two things
-- the child's acceptance of being scapegoated and the need of the
group to have somebody to pick on. This two way process is
important to remember because it means that as a teacher or group
worker you can intervene in either of two ways. You can work
individually with the child who is being scapegoated to help him
conform enough to group norms so that he will be accepted or you can
work with the group as a whole. "Why do you need someone to pick
on?" Or, "What is it about the way we are operating that we have to
shut somebody out, that we have to be mean to somebody?" And,
though it may surprise you, everytime I have gone this second route
the children have become aware and have helped me to become aware of
the fact that, indeed, the group did need somebody to pick on.
(Ways to handle this will be discussed in Chapters 6 and 7.)

If you have questions about this idea, if it does not seem to
ring true, think about some group experiences that you have had
where group members worked well together. Was there somebody who
was different in that group? Why was that person not the butt of
mean jokes? I have worked with many, many classes at all grade

levels in which children who were very different were protected,
liked, even favored by the other class members. I have to wonder
what was different about such a class. Part of the answer may lie
in an individual's acceptance of his own uniqueness, but another
important difference is that the class members felt good enough
about themselves that they could include the deviant member and
find a way to support that person.

There are two other major dysfunctioning roles which might be
considered types of scapegoats but which I want to list separately.
One is the group monopolist, the person who takes over, does all the
talking and does not give the other group members a chance to get a
word in edgewise. Again, the monopolist may be holding forth in a
faculty meeting, a therapeutic group or in a classroom. I cannot
say too strongly that that person cannot monopolize unless the
group is willing to let him. In a well functioning group somebody
who talks endlessly is told by a member or members to be quiet, to
shut up, in a way which is nonrejecting. The behavior is thus
controlled by the group members themselves. If, then, a young
person in a group or faculty is allowed to talk on and on, there is
something in it for the group to let him continue. The last time I
saw this happen was in an adult group when a faculty was extremely
angry with their administrator and yet, for some reason, did not
feel comfortable discussing it with her. Their anger went
underground and they decided it was not safe or worthwhile to
express it openly. One person in the group, however, saw this as an
opportunity to get a great deal of recognition and attention from
the group. He raised an irrelevant issue and began to monopolize,
to take over. The group members were willing to accomodate him as a
way of not having to deal directly with their frustration and
anger.

Another type of group dysfunctioning role is the isolate, the
person who is truly shut out. Now, I do not mean the person who is
merely quiet because a member can be quiet but still be very much a
part of the group. I do mean, however, that some groups, for
various reasons, truly shut somebody out, do not allow that person
to become a part. Such exclusion requires a person allowing
himself to be shut out (maybe because it is too painful to try to
become a part of the group) and the agreement of the group to shut
him out. One therapeutic group in a high school had a core of six
members, and the facilitator, thinking the group was too small,
would occasionally bring in one or two new members. What was
fascinating was that those one or two new members would come once or
twice, the group would be polite to them, but they would never come
back. Perhaps this group was still in the unity stage and did not
want to include anybody else, but for whatever reason, they
isolated any new member and that person did not return. It is
possible, however, to be present and still be an isolate, to be a
member of a class and not be overtly scapegoated but never be
accepted as a viable member of the group.

Scapegoating, isolation, monopoly. All are symptoms of
dysfunctioning in the group. Yet it is typical for a teacher,
therapist or administrator to see only that one person is having a

problem and deal with it strictly at the personal level, rather than viewing it as a group process issue.

Crisis. At certain stages and times during its development, every group goes through crises, which might temporarily convert a malfunctioning group into a well functioning group or the other way around. A group who has had difficulty relating to one another all year may band together to get even with a substitute teacher, to support their own teacher if that teacher is ill or unhappy or to respond to some common outside pressure, either positive or negative. I was in a class that got pegged as a "bad class," one which did not cooperate with each other. The students' joint anger at being so pegged pulled them together. A type of pseudo-intimacy developed around a common enemy. On the other hand, there may be a group which has functioned well all year that has a momentary crisis. One junior high group found that they all did very poorly on the U.S. Constitution test. Because the students felt so badly about that, because they were so upset and angry and because they had no outlet for these feelings (except against the teacher whom they loved), they turned on each other as a way of coping. For the first time that year they began to pick on each other, to scapegoat, and to function in ways that were alien to the way they had been functioning in the past. Once the teacher was able to understand the reason for the negative behavior, she helped get the group back to functioning positively.

Most crises lead to transitional role assignments -- the group as a whole functions transitionally in a way which is different from its usual way of operating. This is an important principle to remember so that you do not view the positive or negative functioning of your group members as they revolve around a common crisis, as necessarily continuing once the crisis is over. If the behavior is positive, however, you can certainly build on it as you continue working with your group.

Take a look at some of the groups that you belong to. Do you see the basic maintenance roles operating in those groups? Which are the ones that are dysfunctional and what do you think are some of the causal factors? What role do you feel most comfortable playing? Are you usually a group nurturer, a leader, an enabler? The vast majority of us play different roles depending on what kind of group we are in and our personal investment in the group's purpose. As you begin to explore both yourself and the groups you belong to, you may get a better understanding of how you can be helpful in promoting positive group change.

Cohesiveness. Another component of group process over which a teacher or leader has significant control and which is crucial to developing positive group interaction is group cohesiveness. In any group, whether or not the group "jells," some members develop alliances and affectionate feelings toward each other. In some groups that affection develops primarily in pairs or small subgroups. In a cohesive group, however, members have a warm feeling not only toward each other but toward the group as a whole. Cohesion results from the intensity of the members' involvement with the group.

Cohesion within a group does not usually develop on its own, but rather is greatly affected by how the leader participates, positively or negatively, in the group process. The more cohesive the group the greater the influence on its members. To the extent that a group is attractive to its members it has the capacity to produce changes in attitudes and behavior. In a cohesive class the normative behavior prescribed by the class is much more enforceable than in a noncohesive class. For this reason, one of a teacher's best resources for discipline and classroom management is developing a spirited, cohesive class which will help set limits and support one another.

Conflict. Another component of group process is how a group deals with conflict. Whether or not a group is cohesive, there are bound to be areas of disagreement and the resolution of the conflict becomes important to the general feelings of the members about the group as a whole. There can be cooperation or collision of roles, norms and values as a group attempts to resolve differences.

In some groups, members tend to take sides on important issues. There are two reasons for the polarization of basic differences in groups. One is connected with personal or content issues and the other is related to process issues. The first, most obvious and easiest to deal with, is when there are genuine differences of opinion, when people who like and trust each other find themselves disagreeing about a content issue and yet trust each other to resolve it. How these issues are resolved depends a great deal, of course, on the stage of development that the group is in.

The more subtle difference of opinion or source of conflict is within the group process itself. This is particularly true for the group that dichotomizes on two sides of the fence on the same issue. Because most educational issues create some ambivalence in every person involved, the dichotomy tends to reflect the other side of the ambivalence of each group member. I was leading a workshop for teachers a few months ago on Humanizing Education -- how teachers could be more responsive to the needs of their pupils. The majority of the teachers were extremely receptive and very flexible in trying to adapt their teaching methods to the needs of the pupils with whom they worked. However, there was one "Old Guard" teacher (though he was a relatively young man) who challenged everything I said, telling me that he felt that this new humanizing of education was destructive and that we really needed to go back to the old use of the "rod" as an enforcement agent. He said he believed that if you gave pupils what they wanted they would walk all over you. As we continued our discussion he became polarized at the opposite end of the other teachers who were all very permissive and "giving."

It was clear to me that the majority of the other teachers were really not being honest with themselves - that there is a piece of every teacher that says, "Doggone it, why don't these kids shape up

and do what I tell them? I'm tried of being so nice and giving all
the time." The young man who was challenging all of us in talking
about the "old way" and how pupils should be forced to respect
adults was really speaking, not only for himself, but for that
piece of every teacher in the room. I did not doubt that piece was
there, but as long as he said it for them, they could come across as
"good guys". I dealt with this by asking each teacher to think
about the part of them that would like the students to be obedient,
"What would it be like if students complied with your every
request?" After initial resistance to this task, they shared the
other side of their ambivalence, the piece that said, "Gee, life
would be a lot simpler if only the children would just do what we
told them to." As they began to speak to that side of their own
ambivalence, the young man who had been so attacking and
challenging all of a sudden began to mellow and said, "You know,
kids aren't really that bad. They're not as bad as I said they
were. I really do listen to them. I'm not as mean as I say, but
you guys are just too soft." We gradually agreed that each teacher,
being who she is, needs to cope with her own ambivalence about how
students should be treated.

Roles, norms, group cohesion and conflict -- all are components of group process. Whether you are intervening at the content, personal or process level, these factors will have great
impact, one way or the other, on the group as a system.

Chapter Three

WHAT MAKES GROUPS WORK

As I have become increasingly able to understand how groups operate, it has become clear that there are many and varied factors, internal and external, which affect group process. Some of these elements are outside of the power of the leader and members. Many, however, can be controlled. This appears to be particularly true if the leader has some control over the way the group begins initially. As an educator, it is important for you to differentiate for yourself what power you have and what is beyond your control.

I have consulted in numerous school systems with teachers, administrators and pupil personnel team members around group issues. Usually I have been asked to assist with a group that was floundering. As I studied "what went wrong" I saw a pattern emerge which elucidated some of the factors which appear crucial to group performance. My thought was that if I could isolate these elements which were destructive, I might be able to formulate a conceptual structure of what it takes to make groups work. Continuing in my attempt to move from what went wrong to how to make groups go right, I found my consultation moving from a problem solving focus to a preventative one. For the past several years I have been testing these formulations against actual groups - classroom and therapeutic, natural and formed - and have been able to find several consistent criteria for what it takes to make groups become cohesive, well-functioning units.

Compatible Goals

Perhaps the most important element in creating a positive group experience is the merging of purposes of why that group exists. The multiple goals of the variety of group members, of the group leader and of the sponsoring school must be compatible. If these goals do not somehow mesh together the group is doomed before it starts. Now that does not mean that the goals have to be the same, but they must be able to live together. In a teachers' association there were some teachers who were power hungry, who needed to be recognized, who needed to be valued and who very much wanted to take a strong leadership role to satisfy their personal needs. Other teachers in that group were interested in getting more pleasant working surroundings and higher salaries, while still others looked for group cohesion and closeness with one another. Now, these sets of goals, while they are very different, are compatible. They can live together. One group may say to another, "Okay, you can have the power. We will help you feel important and significant if you will also keep our interests in mind."

Another teachers' association in the same state, however, had incompatible goals. Some teachers just wanted to be left alone, to be able to shut their classroom doors and not have to relate to the school or other faculty very much beyond that. Other teachers were attempting to organize and have everybody rally around a couple of common causes which they felt were extremely important. There were two or three other teachers who were so embittered that all they wanted to do was retaliate for the pain and hurt they had experienced. Those teachers' need to retaliate was incompatible with the goals of the teachers who needed to withdraw. Nor did either set of goals fit with those of the teachers who were fighting constructively for a common cause. Because of such incompatible goals among the members, that particular teachers' association turned inward on each other, everyone got angry and little was accomplished that school year.

In another high school I was called in to "put out the fire" that had been created by incompatible goals. A high school principal was concerned about the number of young people in the school who were smoking marijuana. He called in the school social worker and said, "Let's start a group of these young people who are using pot." His goal, obviously, though it was unspoken, was to get the young people to stop using marijuana. The social worker, who was frustrated because he had not been able to get many of the young people involved in his practice replied, "I would like, if I could, to get these kids to talk about their feelings. If they only talked about their feelings, the group would be a satisfying experience for me and helpful to the students because they obviously are running away from their problems." The young people, when they were approached about being in what affectionately became known as the "Pot Group," said, "Well, we don't think there's anything wrong with us, but we would love to get together with people who are also smoking pot." Their motivation was to find a cheaper and better source of supply of drugs.

These are obviously incompatible goals. The young people who wanted to use the group as a drug source had different goals than the school who wanted to stop the pot smoking. Even the social worker, with all of his good intentions, who said, "Talk about your feelings," clashed with the goals of the school and the members. A crisis occurred when one night the group (meeting in a member's apartment without the worker) was arrested by the police for smoking marijuana. They told the police that the group was being sponsored by the school. School administrators were called, parents became involved and it was a very messy situation. It was then that I was called in to find out why that group had become so destructive. It was clear to me that the difficulty was caused by faulty structure based on incompatible goals.

But it is possible to have compatible goals between students and teachers or among student-social worker-administrator. Had the social worker mentioned above been more knowledgeable about groups, he might have been able to find a type of group where the goals would have meshed better. Such a group was composed of fifth grade boys, all of whom had trouble sitting still. They created hassles for the teacher, who finally suggested that they be in a group with the school psychologist to see if there were better ways to control their behavior. The psychologist's goal was to discover with these

boys what it was that made it so hard for them to concentrate and
sit still. Was it something inside themselves or something in the
classroom or a combination? This goal was compatible with the
teacher's goal of stopping the behavior. She felt if the
psychologist could tell her why the boys behaved in that manner,
she might be able to help them act more appropriately. The boys
said, "Sure, we'll be in the group - it will be good to get out of
the class." When the psychologist explained the goal of helping
the boys understand and change their behavior, they agreed to be in
the group if they got out of class. This was a compatible set of
goals, even though each was very different from the other. That
group turned out to be a very positive experience for all
concerned. As the boys began to have somebody outside the class
listen to how they felt, and as the psychologist and the boys began
to understand some of the reasons behind the acting out, their
behavior in the classroom changed and the teacher mellowed. This
success was based primarily on their sharing of goals.

If you are a part of any group that is having difficulty you
might ask yourself if the problem is one of incompatible goals. If
it is a classroom group, what are the teacher's goals? What are the
school's goals? And what are the students' goals? If it is a
therapeutic group, what are your goals as a leader? The agency's
goals? The members' goals? How can they all fit together? Your
ability to merge these goals increases the likelihood of a
successful group experience for each member as well as the leader.
Ways to help these goals become more compatible will be discussed
in later chapters relevant to the specific age groups.

Group Composition

Group composition is another important part of what makes
groups work. Who are the members? How is the group composed? In a
classroom group frequently the composition is arbitrary and you
have little control. But understanding how the membership fits
together is very important in any event. When you form groups
yourself, either for therapeutic purposes or for task completion,
you will want to think about some group process issues which will
help you form efficient and compatible groups.

There are certain combinations of people which seem to work
well together and others which do not. Before you compose a group
you need to be aware of some general guidelines of composition. As
you select your members, try to make sure that all of the basic
maintenance roles are accounted for - that in your group you have
potentially at least one member who can be a nurturer, a subject
changer, an enabler and a leader. In addition, a group will not
work well if everyone in the group tends to fulfill the same role.
If you have a group of all leaders and no followers, that group is
likely to be in a power struggle from beginning to end. If, on the
other hand, you have a group of people who all nurture a great deal
but are not particularly strong leaders, people may feel good about
each other but never get the task done.

There are some other basic issues with respect to composition
for constructive group process. One is to try to avoid too many

extremes, and if possible, do not put one of anything in a group. Let me explain what I mean. If I had a choice, I would never put one poor child in a group of affluent children, nor one Black child in a group of White children, nor one girl in a group of boys, nor one slightly retarded child in a group of bright children. When one group member is quite different from the others, regardless of what the difference is, that person tends to be a built-in scapegoat and may get picked on or act out for the others. So, whether you are composing a classroom, a therapeutic group or a faculty committee, if you have a choice, try to find enough people who are representative of the various maintenance roles that are needed to form a helpful group and try to avoid setting up a situation which may inherently create one or more scapegoats.

There is another "golden rule" when you are forming a group in a school, i.e., "Avoid putting people with similar symptoms together." That is true regardless of the type of group - whether it is a faculty committee or a therapeutic group of young people in a junior high school. If you put people with similar symptoms together, they will tend to integrate that symptom as a group norm. In addition, groups with members who have a variety of coping mechanisms greatly enrich the opportunities for members to view a variety of alternative behaviors. I was a member of a committee composed of people who all dealt with their frustrations by blaming the administration. We all sat around and complained and nobody did anything to make it better. There was a dramatic change in that committee when we invited two people who were doers rather than complainers, and they said, "Yes, you are right, it is intolerable - what are we going to do about it?" This new, more active approach made all the difference in the world to the functioning of the committee.

In a junior high school, a group of young people was composed in which all of the members had symptoms of restlessness and acting out behavior. That behavior was the only way most of them knew how to express how they felt and their frustration with themselves and with the school. When these youngsters were put together the group became almost unmanageable. If the leader had had a strong behavioral orientation, he might have been able to help the boys stay under control, but they still would have lacked the experience of learning from other young people how to cope with their frustration in different ways.

Now, there is one notable exception to this guildline. That is, there will be times when people with common symptoms want to change that symptom, and therefore putting them into a group for that purpose, because that is what they really want, can be workable. A successful group of sophomore overweight girls was formed of members who all said, one way or another, "I'm fat and ugly and I want to lose weight." The goal of that group was not to get the girls to talk about their feelings but rather to get them to lose weight. It was run cooperatively by a school nurse and a counselor and was very effective. The peer support in losing weight was powerful. If a group with a different purpose had been composed of all overweight girls, then the tendency might have been for the girls to eat together when they felt frustrated with ensuing weight gain.

To summarize some rules of thumb, if you are forming a group yourself, try to avoid one of anything. Try to see that the maintenance roles are fulfillable and try to group people who can agree on some common purpose in meeting and who express their frustrations, hostility, anger and caring in different ways.

Many of you are probably saying, "Are you kidding? I don't have any choice about who is in my classes. This information helps me see what is wrong with a class, but what can I do about it?" There are, indeed, some things that you <u>can</u> do to make things better. If you see a basic maintenance role missing, you may need to fill that role yourself or to help it develop within the group. One teacher enlisted the aid of a lonely boy to help with the nurturing. She asked him to keep an eye out for children who seemed unhappy. This exciting task not only aided the boy's self-esteem, but also it provided a valuable service to the group. You can do much to help students work well together. This task is not easy but the results can be extremely rewarding.

Role of the Leader

Another factor to consider in helping make groups work is the role of the worker or teacher. What function does he or she fulfill? How does he do it? However the leader operates must be compatible with the reason the group exists. If I came to you and said, "I'm here to help you learn about groups," and then sat around offering no suggestions, you would quickly become frustrated with me. The way I was operating would sabotage the reason that we were meeting. The same goes for the classroom. If you have a classroom meeting for the purpose of giving the children a chance to express their concerns and assume responsibility for what goes on in the classroom, your actions must support that goal. One teacher told her children, "I want you to be more responsible," yet every time one of the children made a suggestion she attacked it as unworkable. Her actions negated the very goal she was trying to achieve.

In a therapeutic group with a behavorial emphasis, the goal was to try to get the children to take more responsibility for going to school. The leaders found that reinforcing appropriate behavior worked well, but when they slipped into talking with the children about how they felt rather than, "What can we do to get you to school?", the school attendance dropped again. I am sure that you can think of many situations where the way a leader functioned negated the reason the group was meeting.

Permissable Content

Another factor important to group functioning is the content. What is okay to talk about? What is being discussed? How does the content support or undermine the reason the groups is meeting? If you are having a meeting of a social club with people from diverse political background, you may need to prohibit discussions of politics in order to keep the session sociable. A group of children preparing for a pageant had to agree to limit their discussion to pageant issues so they could get the task completed. What is permissable in terms of content needs to support why the group is meeting.

Use of Feelings

Still another factor is how feelings are used within the group process. In some groups, feelings are very, very important as a part of the process of engagement. In other groups, primarily those which are task oriented, if people sit around and talk about how they feel the job may never get done. There are times in class when discussing feelings is very appropriate and other times when such discussions get in the way of learning. How are feelings used in your group at school? Are they supported or disregarded? How does that fit with the reason your group is meeting? If you are going to have a cohesive faculty, feelings are very important and being able to express them openly to each other is extremely valuable. Ways to use feelings to enhance group process will be discussed throughout the book.

Use of Group Process

I also take a look at how the process itself is addressed by the leader when a group is operating. Since it is clear that process is going on all of the time, the question is how much do you talk about it? How much do you deal with process issues? How much do you try to affect them? It is important to realize that how the group process is used or not used is very relevant to the success of a group.

This formulation of compatible goals, role of the leader, good composition, use of content, use of feelings and use of group process is highly important to keep in mind when considering any group. If all of these factors support the reason that the group is meeting, then the group will probably be successful in its task. If, on the other hand, one or more do not, then the group is in trouble before it ever begins. Think about some of the groups to which you belong. Which of these factors operate in a way that support the purpose of the group? Which do not? What would you change if you could? How?

Four Essential Qualities

Moving from our knowledge of what makes groups work, it is often a question about why, and when, people want to belong to a group. What are some of the qualities essential to voluntary participation in any group? What entices someone to decide to participate in group interaction? As I have studied groups it has become clear that the qualities necessary for an individual to participate in a group are the very same qualities as those needed in a classroom for students to want to learn. These qualities are many and varied and some differ from community to community and from person to person. Every socioeconomic and ethnic group represented in the schools with which I have worked has some different expectations of groups within their subculture   and

differing values to their members. But there are four qualities
which are consistently required for someone to want to participate.
The way these qualities are requested and acted out may differ
greatly, but the qualities themselves are universal.

   Safety. For anyone to want to participate in a group it needs
to be a safe place to be. By that I mean both emotionally and
physically safe for everyone present. In a school where knives and
guns are prevalent, it may not be physically safe to set foot in the
classroom, or the school at all, and peoples' fear will greatly
inhibit learning. On the other hand, the fear in a classroom which
is not emotionally safe also has strong inhibiting factors to
learning and to group participation. In any unsafe group, the goal
moves from participation to survival, and the energies and efforts
of the participants are focused to that end - survival. I wish I
had a quarter for every time I have talked with a teacher who said,
"My only goal is to survive the rest of the school year." There are
many reasons why a classroom or school is not a safe place to be,
emotionally or physically or both. This book attempts to help
everyone who comes in contact with groups assist in making those
groups safe.

   You may think I am putting too much emphasis on this quality,
that adults do not need that much safety, especially emotional
safety. You may feel that adults can take care of themselves. And
yet I wonder what it would be like if you and I were sitting across
from each other in a group session and I had encouraged you to be
open and the first time you asked a question, I ridiculed you.
Perhaps I said,"Boy, that was the dumbest question I have ever
heard! Any more stupid questions?" That interaction might have
caused some of you to get your dander up and fight back and say,
"Hey, you can't talk like that to us!" If you did that, I might
back down or again try to "put you in your place." My hunch is that
the majority of you would do as I would have done - shut up and say
to myself, "I better keep my mouth shut in this group; it is not
safe to open it." Then, if I had a chance I would probably leave at
the first opportunity.

   Another interesting dynamic about group safety is that if the
group is not safe for everyone it is safe for no one. If I put you
down, not only would the group be unsafe for you, but for the other
group members as well. If I can do it to you, I can do it to them.
They might think, "Forget it, I'm not going to risk either." This
dynamic occurs in classrooms, faculty meetings and other groups of
all kinds in schools. Time after time I have seen safety be a core
issue.

   Safety, or lack of safety, of course, comes not only from the
teacher, leader or facilitator to the group member but also exists
among the members themselves. If a bully in a group makes it unsafe
for another member and if that is allowed to continue, the group
becomes unsafe for everyone there, including the bully. If group
members feel safe with one another, they protect each other from
attack, from the leader or other sources. As leaders, therapists,
teachers, principals, whatever your role is in the school system,

you need to help the school be a safe place.

   Something for you. Another dimension that makes one want to participate in a group, which is almost as important as emotional and physical safety, is that a group must have something in it for the members. If I am going to risk myself in my learning, or in talking about myself or in my teaching, there must be something in it for me to do so. One of the first things that everybody asks, whether they think about it consciously or not, is, "What's in it for me? What do I get back for me for making this investment?" In some classrooms what students get back is teacher or parent approval, or high grades, and these are certainly of value. But there are additional things students can get for themselves out of learning. You may want to do some thinking about how you (being who you are) can help students make an investment in their learning. How can they get something back for themselves in addition to grades and approval? One of my prime goals as a teacher is to help each student find something that he can get excited about in whatever it is that I am teaching. This makes the learning inherently useful instead of depending upon external recognition or rewards. I have what I call the "selfish approach" to learning and teaching. Everybody, including the teacher, ought to get something for himself out of every learning experience.

   Now that is somewhat idealistic and there are courses, and some parts of most courses, that are not going to be exciting. Some material you have to learn just because you have to know it, and some content which is exciting to some students is boring to others. But, hopefully, this is the exception to the rule. When the prevailing focus of a teacher is on motivating and exciting the children about their learning, the more boring learning tasks do not loom so large. Other groups are also faced with unpleasant tasks at times, but you should not expect any member of a committee, any member of a therapeutic group, any member of a class or anybody playing on the playground to participate constructively in the group unless there is something they get back for themselves - that is normal, that is natural, that is necessary, and I think kind of nice.

   Something to contribute. After the sales pitch I just gave you might be surprised at the next quality that must be there for people to participate actively in a group. Every person in every group should feel they have something to contribute. It is not enough to just take. A group member must feel that he has something to give. I vividly remember meeting with some high school students who had been in a treatment group for the majority of their junior year. As we reviewed at the end of the year what it was that made the group so successful in the eyes of the members, a consistent response (which each gave in his own way) was, "When I joined this group, I felt pretty crummy about myself, but when I found that I could be helpful to other people - could give advice and support when other people were hurting - I knew I wasn't as bad as I thought I was." This ability to give to other people turned out to be one of the prime curative factors of that group.

This is not necessarily the case in every group nor for all
people. Many of you have had members in your group or class who did
not seem to <u>want</u> to give. One teacher described two such students,
"They don't <u>want</u> to give. They just think about themselves. They
don't care about anybody else!" It is very difficult to work with
people who appear to have that attitude, but it is important to find
creative ways to help them give, if you can, for them and for you.
I worked with a group of delinquents who "ripped off" everybody and
everything in sight and whose negative feelings about themselves
and others led to pretending they did not care about anything. When
they were hired to manage a shelter for injured animals, this
antagonistic attitude turned to one of deep concern. Discovery of
their ability to give lessened their need to act out.

We have a responsibility as teachers, or other school personnel, not only to see that our group participants get something for
themselves but also that everybody contributes something.
Sometimes this is harder than seeing that everyone gets something,
but it is even more important.

<u>Someone cares</u>. A final important quality is that every member
in a group has to know that somebody cares whether he is there or
not. As one teacher said, "There's nothing worse than being gone
for a week with the flu and nobody noticed that you were gone." All
of us need warm, caring relationships, both on and off the job, in
and out of the classroom, whether we are teachers, administrators
or students. One of the things that makes it so hard for the young
person in a classroom who is being scapegoated is that he feels that
no one cares and therefore makes little investment in trying to get
people to like him. Besides that, he probably does not like himself
much either. My experience is that when caring can come through,
when I am able to show a person who has no friends that <u>I</u> care, if
indeed I do, then he has reason to think that he might be likable
after all, and may begin to care about himself, even just a little.

Striking a Balance

But no group, no class, can <u>always</u> have all four things at one
time. No class or group can always be safe, always have something
in it for everyone, help everybody contribute and help everyone
feel cared for and significant. It is just not possible. I have
found, however, that when those qualities are usually present, when
the group is constructively functioning, then during those rocky
times when one or more qualities is missing, one of the others
temporarily makes up the loss. In my own group treatment there were
times when it was pretty scary, when it was not safe. At those
times the caring that I experienced from the other members made
that lack of safety temporarily manageable. Every one of you has,
at one time or another, sat through a boring, difficult lecture or
class where there was absolutely nothing in it for you, but still
you were required to be there. Perhaps you were able to tolerate it
because you were sitting next to somebody you cared about with whom
you exchanged complaining notes. I have gotten through many a
faculty meeting or dull committee meeting by sitting with somebody
I liked.

Teacher As Group Leader

In the training that I do with teachers I try to help them find ways to build these four qualities into their classes. They need to work with the process and personal issues as well as the content level of interaction. Teachers often learn to set aside much of the first two or three weeks of the school year for process issues. Since the first two or three weeks tend to be the time when the norms are set and roles and goals are established for the rest of the year, group process is of particular importance at that time. During this period a teacher needs to ask many process questions. How can we work together? How can each of you get something for yourselves out of being in this class? What do each of you have to contribute that you think is unique and unusual? What roles do you play in other groups? How many teachers take the opportunity to say, "Okay, kids, let's make this year different. I'd like your learning to be exciting and fun for you and for all of us to work together. What are some expectations for behavior that we can agree on that will support that goal?" The teacher, by facilitating the decision-making process becomes an ally with the group to help it function in a cooperative manner.

A number of you may be saying, "Two weeks! It is just too much time! I have material I must cover. If I try this my students will be academically way behind." A small study was done in a number of fifth and sixth grade classes. One group of teachers spent the first two to three weeks of class focusing primarily, but not exclusively, on helping each member of the class feel significant and helping the group as a system develop constructively by working on process issues. In addition, throughout the school year, group process issues took precedence over the lesson for the day. A control group of classes was more traditionally managed. The teacher set the rules, saying, "Here's the way it is going to be." The children (as usual) tested the rules and the teacher, and the focus was primarily on content issues. The major research question was whether or not this intense focus on process the first few weeks of class would mean less cognitive learning on the part of the students. Both sets of students were tested at the end of November and again in June on their cognitive learning as well as their attitude toward school. The findings of that November testing showed that most of the children who were involved in the process classes were more positive about school and assumed more responsibility for what went on in the classroom than did the children in the traditional setting. The children in the traditional setting, however, at the end of November, led in retention of specific cognitive material. When the school year was over, however, the children in the process classrooms had surpassed the traditional class members in cognitive learning as well as maintaining their positive attitudes and behavior in school. This small, informal unpublished study supports my own observations that when children are involved in the process of their learning, they not only feel better about school and become more responsible students, but retain more of their "book learning" as well.

Let me say first of all what I am <u>not</u> proposing. I am not suggesting that the classroom be turned over to the children,

regardless of their age.   Children need a strong leader/teacher.
Nor am I proposing that we become permissive and let children run
all over everybody.   It is interesting that I am considered a very
strict teacher even though I almost never punish.   My strictness is
my   insistence   that   every   member   of   that   class   assume   some
responsibility   for   helping   keep   the   class   a   good   learning
environment.   When something goes wrong, I stop the class until we
can   set   it   right   again.   Instead   of   assuming   all   of   the   responsibility myself, I share it with my students.   How you do this,
if indeed you want to, varies greatly depending on the age of your
students,   who   you   are   as   a   teacher   and   what   makes   you   feel   good
about yourself.   The specifics, age-related, will come in following
chapters.

Other Applications

     While this discussion has been related mostly to the class-
room, the same dynamics are easily transferable to any other group
within a school.   I wonder how many PTA presidents have thought of
dealing with their dwindling attendance by asking all members to
come   to   one   meeting   to   discuss   how   to   make   it   a   more   viable
experience for everyone.   How many principals, when things begin to
go sour on the faculty give them the task of making it better for
themselves.   To do this a principal runs the risk of getting honest
"feed-back" from the faculty about things he might be doing which
get in the way of positive group functioning.   (One of the problems
of asking people what they think is that they might tell you.)   My
experience in a variety of settings shows that insistence on mutual
assumption of responsibility and decision-making is very important.

     Your response to this discussion may well be, "It sounds very
nice but what if it doesn't work?   And what about the times that I
get   so   angry   I   don't   want   to   be   rational?"   These   are   good
questions.   You may want to find new ways to get yourself out of a
bind you are in as well as try to stay out of the bind in the first
place.   As a teacher, I have my classes trained.   If I temporarily
lose control of myself or my feelings, or become irresponsible or
irrational, the students not only let me know it, but they help me
out.   Even   second   graders   can   say,   "Hey,   Mrs.   Johnson,   you're
yelling again."   That can be a signal to me to take a look at what I
am upset about.   By sharing that with my class, I can then help them
see what it is they are doing that gets me so angry.   Then we can
discuss what we can do about it to have a better day together.
There is a process, a structure for doing this that has been helpful
to me when my own feelings get in the way or when I come up against
a problem.   The next chapter will discuss this problem solving
process.

Chapter Four

THE PROBLEM SOLVING PROCESS: YOUR ALLY

One of the principles of "Human Education" is that children
and teachers are important human beings. Each is unique, special,
and very human. Many schools give permission to children to be
human, including the right to err. How many schools, however, see
the teacher as having the right to make mistakes? One teacher
bitterly stated, "I spend all day accepting both the strengths and
weaknesses of the children in my class. I teach them, nurture them,
value them and help them learn from their mistakes. When is someone
going to care about me? Why can't I make mistakes as the children
do? I'm human too!"

Teachers do make mistakes, of course, as do administrators,
psychologists, social workers, consultants and all other people.
The very human qualities which cause errors are the same that make
teachers so responsive to the children. The ability to become
involved with the children you serve is a great strength, and yet it
leaves you vulnerable to be hurt, to let your feelings get in the
way, to err.

The problem solving process* is not for anyone who is perfect.
It was designed to be used by those of us who make more mistakes
than we choose to admit. Basically, it is an approach to problem
resolution to use when difficulties occur between you and any other
person or group of people within the school. The process assumes
that most real problems are two-way, that both you and the other
party are responsible. This means that you also have the power to
use this process to change the way things are, to resolve the
problem in some way or another.

Problem Definition
The first step in the problem solving process is to define the
various parts of the problem as you perceive them. What is wrong?
What happened? How did it happen? How do you feel about what
happened? What did it do to you as a person to have had this
experience? You need to try to get in touch not only with the
content of the problem and the process of how it happened but also
your personal response to it. Hopefully, then, you can move beyond
that to questions about the other people involved. What do you
think happened to them personally? How do they feel?

----

*This process draws on basic conflict resolution techniques from
many theories. It was developed by myself and my friend,
colleague, co-therapist and co-trainer, Peter Sternberg (Child
Therapist at Lake County Mental Health Center, Illinois). Most of
the ideas were conceptualized together, but much of the material on
creative use of fantasies is uniquely his.

One teacher kept a whole class after school because they had become "smart alecky" and defiant. Usually she could handle such an occurrence and settle the children down without becoming punitive. But this particular day she was feeling rotten physically, she had had a disagreement with her husband before school, and the material which she had so carefully ordered for her lesson plan had not arrived. The combination of all of these aggravations, plus the obnoxious behavior of some of the children in the class, made her feel furious, sorry for herself, frustrated and helpless. She was certainly entitled to those feelings. Her affective response was very real and relevant to the situation. But she felt badly about the way she had blamed and punished the children and asked me to help her understand what had happened. This incident had brought out a side of her she did not like very much.

Sometimes keeping children after school can be helpful, but in this instance the teacher perceived it as her attempt to get even because the children had made her feel so badly. When I encouraged her to take a look at the problem in its entirety, supporting her feelings both from within and without the classroom as being an important part of her, we were then able to move to another question. How could she help the children understand what had happened and regain a nonpunitive attitude in the classroom?

Feelings and Fantasies

The second stage of the problem solving process is to accept your feelings and allow yourself to experience what you would like to do. When the teacher was so angry, for instance, what would she have liked to do? Clearly, in this case, a part of the teacher wanted to get even because the pupils had hurt her feelings. Her desire to get even was perfectly natural. Many teachers, when they have been hurt, have vivid fantasies of methods of retaliation and relish them! Having fantasies is usually harmless yet potentially very helpful -- it is what you do that matters.

I would like to digress a moment to talk about the tremendous therapeutic value for people within a school system of permitting themselves to have wild fantasies about ways to cope with disquieting situations. Fantasies do not cost anything, do not hurt and can help a teacher experience her own legitimate feelings. Perhaps the teacher in the above illustration, had she allowed herself, would have fantasized some wicked way to get even with those demons in her class. One teacher used to enjoy fantasizing hanging pupils from the coat hooks in the closet. She never did but the fantasy helped her through some rough times with difficult children. Do not be afraid to have negative fantasies as well as positive ones and to allow yourself to experience your feelings.

Stop

Once you know what the problem is, once you know how you feel about it and have allowed yourself a fantasy, stop. Just stop. This is the third step in the problem solving process. That pause gives you a change to regain your equilibrium. Then, without

giving up the relevance of your feelings, try to move beyond them
and think about what it is that you would really like to have
happen. What kind of rapport would you like to have with those
young people? What kind of a relationship do you really want with
your faculty if you are a principal? And in that stopping process,
when your feelings are very evident and appreciated, but put aside
for a few moments, you can set specific goals for what you would
like to have happen next.

A word of caution. The goals you set must be limited enough so
that they are attainable if you act in a different way. You cannot
take a child who makes you furious because he continues to say how
much he hates school and have as your goal to make him love school.
This is obviously not realistic. But you may very well be able to
take a small piece of that unrealistic goal and say, "Okay, if he
hates school and I want him to like it, I'd like to start with
finding out if we can have one good experience together in the
classroom. Can we have a good day, or a good lesson, any one time
that both of us would enjoy to set the tone for other things to
come?"

Plan of Action

After you have set your limited goal you then need to move to
Step Four, which is to develop a plan of action to attain that goal.
Ask yourself, "If my goal is to help this youngster have a positive
experience with me and for me to enjoy him, what are some of the
things I can do to help that come about?"

This is the time when you may want to pick up those feelings
again which you put aside in the "stop" phase and consider whether
there is some way to use those feelings in a way to achieve your
goal. Your plan of action should include helping the other people
involved understand some of the things they did that upset you and
what you can all do to improve things.

You, for example, in your anger and frustration at the boy who
hates school might take him aside and share your frustration with
him. Without blaming him you can let him know that you are
frustrated and he must be too. You two can then develop together a
plan to try something new. Is it possible for us to have a good
morning tomorrow? What could each of us do to enjoy our morning?
This conversation might lead to some partialized, workable goals,
agreeable to both student and teacher. The teacher who is so angry
with her class that she becomes punitive may be able to use her
anger in a helpful way. She might tell the class how angry she is,
not blaming them, but as a way to get them involved. She can then
ask them how they feel. What would they like different? After this
mutual sharing of feelings the students and teacher can put
together what each of them can do to change the situation, or be
ready for it if it begins to happen again.

A Built-In Contingency Plan

The Fifth Step in the problem solving process is what I call
the "escape hatch". Suppose you get in touch with your feelings,

you stop, you set a goal, you make a plan of action and it falls
flat. That is always a risk, so your next step is to ask, prior to
putting your plan of action to work, "What if ...?" What if the
plan does not work? What if the child does not come? What if I
cannot control my feelings? In this way you build in a contingency
plan, which you can hold in reserve for use as necessary (as you
would take a spare tire on an auto trip in case you need it).

This contingency plan is a means by which most of your problem
solving can be in some way successful, even if your plan of action
does not work out the way you had originally intended. You will
find as you begin to use this model that, in most instances, some of
it works and some of it does not, and your contingency plan may help
you cope with any negative outcomes.

Postponing Action

This problem solving model works best when you are aware
enough of your own feelings that you can creatively and spontane-
ously go through the process, which may take anywhere from 30
seconds to 30 minutes. There will be times, however, when your
feelings are too intense, when you have been hurt too deeply, when
you care too much to use this framework at the time. You may be too
angry to care what the child thinks at that moment. You may be too
hurt by another teacher to be able to understand how she feels.
These are the times when the process needs to be put aside for a
while. At these moments, the best you can do, and the most helpful
thing you can do, is to acknowledge to yourself and to the people
you are working with that you feel too intensely to make a decision
right now about anything. That temporary inability to act is okay.
In fact, when you feel that intensely it is best not to act until
things are in better perspective for you.

One teacher, who had been called filthy names by a group of
angry students, felt she had to act. She had tried very hard to
reach these young people and their abusive language hurt and upset
her so much that she knew to talk with them at that point would not
be helpful to her or to the children. Instead, she said, "Kids,
right now my feelings are so strong that I can't talk to you without
saying some things I might be sorry I said. You've hurt me deeply
and we need to take a look at this and see what we're going to do
about it. But I can't do it now. Come back after school, all four
of you, and let's all sit down and see if we can figure out together
what happened and how we can keep this from happening again. I
don't like being hurt and I don't think you do either."

Now even that amount of objectivity showed a great deal of
ability on the part of the teacher to share her feelings in a
helpful way. Many of us cannot even say that much. We may just
have to say, "Go away right now, I can't talk to you. Come back
after school." Or, "I'll talk to you tomorrow." There are many
ways a teacher or principal can create "cooling off time".
Sometimes it helps to ask the group of young people to write down
what they think happened, using the time that they are writing as
space to recoup, to get in touch with your feelings and to get back
into the problem solving process.

A Classroom Example

The problem solving process can be used not only by a teacher to help herself but also as a tool to help herself and a class out of a bind. I used this process with a class of ninth graders who began to attack me for talking beneath them. They said I was treating them like babies. I got very defensive because I felt they were unfair, but I also thought a piece of what they were saying was probably right. I turned on myself, saying, "If I were a better teacher this wouldn't have happened." How many of you do that to yourselves? Do you ever feel that there is something wrong with you as a teacher when things go awry? I doubt if I am the only person who does that to herself time after time.

In any event, because I was hooked into that self-blaming routine and knew it, I realized any response I gave would be angry, apologetic or defensive and that none of these would be particularly helpful. So what I asked the students to do before I shared any of my own feelings was to sit down right then and write a paragraph of what they thought had just happened. Not who was to blame, not whose fault it was, but what happened? At first they were disgruntled about the task, thinking I was going to use it to attack them, and each one tried to blame someone else for starting it. I then suggested that we not use names or blame anyone but just see if we could figure out what happened that got us into this struggle. While they were writing their paragraphs I had a chance to sit at my desk, get angry, feel sorry for myself and have a delicious fantasy about getting up, walking out of the room and getting myself a hot fudge sundae. At that moment I did not care if I ever came back. Then I was able to say, "Okay, stop. What is it that I really want?" What I really wanted was to touch bases with those young people again. Allowing myself to go through that process, to experience my feelings of guilt and anger, to have a marvelous fantasy and then to move beyond that to what did I really want, was very freeing.

When we reconvened, I first had the young people share their paragraphs in small groups. Then each group gave a report, which we put on the blackboard in an attempt to reach a consensus of what had happened. Using this approach, I did not know who had said what, which made the students feel safer. To my surprise I found that their perception of what had happened was almost identical to mine. In addition, they took more responsibility for their part of it than I had expected they would. That allowed us, then, to move to the development of a plan of action so that such an incident would not happen again. Our contingency plan, our Step Five, was, "Okay, we'll try not to let it happen again, but what if it does? What will we do then?" We selected several possibilities for that contingency. After the process was over the class said that what we had done was very helpful and suggested, "Next time Mrs. Johnson gets her feelings hurt, let's go through all the steps again."

Later in the year with that same class, after we had become more trusting of each other and more cohesive, I was able to share with them my first feelings during that incident and what I had done with them. At that point we got excited together about the use of

this problem solving approach with children as well as with adults.
Many of the students quickly grabbed hold of it for use in possible
future confrontations they might have with other students and
faculty.

Evaluation of Outcome

It is an impossible task to understand all of the things that
go on in groups and also keep in touch enough with your own feelings
and desires to be able to always use yourself in a helping way.
Indeed, if you <u>must</u> succeed in order to feel good about your
interventions, if they <u>must</u> work out the way you planned, then you
may be frequently disappointed. In my own work in the schools with
faculty and administrators I have discovered that in order for this
problem solving approach to work, I have to change the way I
evaluate myself. I used to evaluate my decisions and actions based
on how successful I was at getting the outcome I desired. If noise
was a problem in my class, I evaluated my success as a teacher by
how quiet I was able to get the children to be. I do not do that
anymore. Now I evaluate myself, not by the specific outcome, but by
how much I am able to help the students in my class and myself find
some common goal which all of us can support. This plan may not be
the same as I might develop on my own but it is usually more
successful because it was created by all of us togther. I must,
then, change my usual investment from the <u>end result</u> to the <u>process
by which it takes place</u>.

There are times, of course, when the end result becomes
crucial and the process much less important. These are times when
safety is involved, when prompt obedience and response is needed or
when the outcome is particularly important to the teacher or
principal. If you are primarily a process person who lets your
staff, students or therapeutic group participate in the problem
solving process, the times that you have to say, "This is what it
<u>must</u> be, you <u>must</u> follow me now," the group members will usually do
so because they know you would not ask if it was not important.
Since they have not needed in the past to act out against your
authority, they probably will not need to now.

A further dimension involves how I evaluate myself overall as
a teacher. As always, my prime measure is how much my students
learn. But in other ways I find I have to evaluate myself differently than I used to. I no longer can judge myself as a teacher
by how perfect I am and how few mistakes I make. Instead, I
evaluate myself based on how responsive I was to the class or to the
staff. How well was I able to hear their point of view? How much
was I able to facilitate the respect for each other's rights, both
theirs and mine? If I got into a power struggle, how quickly was I
able to perceive that I was in a conflict with a student or students
or other staff? How able was I to accept my piece of the power
struggle? How willing was I to be flexible so that it could be
resolved? All of these questions are relevant to successful use of
the problem solving process in your work within a school system.

Chapter Five

CLASSROOM GROUPS OF YOUNG CHILDREN
(KINDERGARTEN THROUGH THIRD GRADES)

Now that I have spent several chapters telling you what goes on in all groups and giving you a structure by which you can observe specific situations, I need to qualify or take back some of what I have said because groups of primary children are very different from groups of older students. Young children, those in kindergarten through second grade, do not usually develop strong groups with specific peer norms. Third graders are often just beginning to have group alliances, and peer pressure is usually not as powerful as in later years. These young students are more likely to react to, adjust to, or act out against the expectations of the significant adults in their lives than fellow classmates.

There are a number of reasons why this is true. Children under the age of seven are still very much in need of, and controlled by, adults. This dependence is not only for physical need fulfillment, but emotional security as well. The satisfaction which comes from having a peanut butter and jelly sandwich with Mom at lunch combines the needs of hunger and caring. Because many young children have not had opportunities to learn how to relate in depth with their peers, they are very likely to concentrate most of their energies in the adult-child relationships. For this reason, praise and criticism have a great deal more meaning when they come from adults than when given by other children.

Because of this preoccupation with the adult world, and the fact that children of this age are just beginning to form their own peer culture, peer norms and peer pressure have not yet developed their full strength. Young children tend to become more invested in parallel play (playing side by side) than they do in groups. Even when they are _in_ groups, they tend to follow a leader, either constructively or destructively, rather than make a group decision, overtly or covertly, about what action will take place.

During the early grades in school, children frequently develop a second part of their identity. The first is established at home, of course, where the basic issues of trust and mistrust are resolved. During the first developmental stages, children have initial feelings of whether or not they are good people and whether the world is a good place to be. The way they are responded to at home has a most significant impact on youngsters at this time which carries over to life outside the family. The child who is beaten at home comes to school expecting the world at school to be punitive as well. The youngster who "rules the roost" during his early years wants to control the classroom too.

During the first years in school, the child must move from the "known" of the home environment to a wider "unknown" place.

Regardless of their initial upbringing and attitude toward life, these children come to school and meet an entirely new set of expectations and goals. Many must learn how to be acceptable in an outside, less protected situation than they had at home. Some of their thoughts about the world and themselves are reinforced or changed as these children struggle to make a place for themselves in a system outside of their family. The child from a deprived home has a new chance to feel significant, and the child from a warm, loving family has a chance to try out his way of relating on other people. The behavior these children exhibit, the support they get, how they succeed or fail in their attempts to develop beginning friendships are all indicators to them of their worth as people.

The Formative Stage

For these reasons, the first three years in school are extremely important, not only to students' learning, but to their basic attitude toward life in general and themselves in particular. An important educational task in work with children in these formative years is to help them find a place for themselves within the classroom and among their peers, as well as to teach them beginning cognitive skills such as reading, writing, listening and understanding (not to mention learning how to follow directions). These children have an opportunity not only to master new skills, but to learn something about themselves and about groups. Those with self-doubts can find new ways to assure that they are worthwhile human beings. The children who begin school thinking they can do no wrong can be helped to discover and accept some of their vulnerabilities. As one first grade teacher said, "There are two children in my class this year with whom I am working intensely. One is a girl who stays by herself and is trying to keep isolated both from her peers and from her learning. She gives up before she begins. I want her to learn to try. The other girl is a good learner who works quickly and does her work well, but breaks into tears every time she makes one small error. Both of these children need to learn to accept themselves and not give up or dissolve." Helping young people learn how to evaluate themselves realistically and still feel adequate as people is one of the hardest, and most important, tasks that a teacher has to accomplish. One of the best ways to do this, of course, is through the content being taught. The two students above will respond most directly when the teacher's comments are about work just completed. She might say to the girl who has dissolved in tears because of a mistake on her paper to go to her desk and find five good things she has done. The other girl might be asked to finish one small part of the assignment so that she can have a sense of accomplishment rather than an ongoing feeling of failure.

Cooperative Learning

There is yet another dimension to the learning that must take place for children in the early grades - setting the stage for later cooperative learning. Most primary grades are moving to excellent individualized learning programs. Children do need to learn at their own speed and to feel unique and special. They also need to learn how to respond to each other in constructive ways.

They can learn how to nurture, to care, to listen, and to communicate honestly - without hitting one another. When these skills are learned in the early grades, they can be transmitted to positive group process in the future. On the other hand, if they are not mastered in these early years, future positive group participation becomes increasingly difficult.

One way which teachers of young children have used to help teach these skills is through small group exercises, beginning with "pairing". Pairing two children together to complete any small task begins the process of learning how to work in groups. The task might be to learn each others names and something about each other. It might be to look at a book together, and then tell the story to another pair of students. It might be an assignment of counting the amount of money in a pile of change, or figuring out together what time it is. These cognitive concepts can be mastered in pairs, and at the same time, the children gain beginning relationship skills.

Pairing has also been used effectively by social workers and special education teachers in classrooms of young children with behavior problems. It has been found that pairing someone who is withdrawn with someone who is more active can offer each child additional alternatives for behavior which are significant when the pairing is accompanied by activities which help the children try out their newly-learned options. One teacher of very young children who had difficulty controlling their behavior decided to try to help her children learn to express their feelings verbally rather than acting them out. That is a big task for six year olds. But this teacher found that many students can master it if activities are developed which are fun and not too complicated. Last year she took some of the most prevalent feelings which she saw acted out in her class and made them into personalities. She gave each feeling a name (being sure to avoid use of names of any of the children in her class). There was Sad Sally, Mad Mark, Silly Susan, Blue Bob, Happy Harry and many others. Each of these "personalities" became real to the children as she told stories about them, articulating the mood which the name represented. She also drew faces on the board to show what they looked like when they felt that way. As the children became excited about meeting these new characters, they learned how to translate their own feelings to the names on the board. She found that if a child could say, "I feel like Mad Mark today," he was less likely to hit out at someone in another way. This program was very successful, not only in controlling behavior but in helping children learn to identify some of the feelings that they were experiencing and some of the ways these feelings became actions. Use of pairing for this program gave each child more individualized time and made the effort to say feelings rather than act them out a two-person project. Each learned to help the other in their attempts to verbalize their responses.

Teaching cooperative learning includes helping children prepare to work in groups. Just as we have activities for "reading readiness" we should consider "group readiness" classroom programs. There are many group experiences which teach young children what

happens in groups and how to be constructive members. By
participating in some of these simple exercises, students can learn
how to communicate with one another and get a taste of what it is
like to be part of a group. Progressive stories are "fun" exercises
which move toward group participation. One student starts a story
and when the teacher claps her hands that child stops, wherever he
is in the tale. Then another student picks up the story where the
other left off. This process continues until many children have
had a chance to add their part to the story, often with hilarious
results. This group story which is so much fun also teaches
children ways to be group members, how to listen, to wait your turn
and to make a contribution to a group effort. If an audio or video
tape is made of the story and the children can listen to it later,
they can also learn about their impact on the finished product. One
second grade girl, for instance, was quite giggly during the story.
When she listened to the tape, she became quiet and subdued.
Without saying another word, her silly disrupting behavior became
much more controlled. Other group projects, which allow these
young creative beings their full individuality include group plays,
pictures and stories about themselves.

Most childrens' readers show children playing one or two at a
time, but not in group interaction. Your students might want to
write a story about what happens on their block after school. How
do they play together? How do decisions get made? How does it
work? Or they might want to put on a play which requires group
effort and then discuss together not only how the play was, but
their thoughts about the way they worked together. I was working
with one second grade class where the children wanted to put on a
play. The girls refused to work with the boys, so they agreed to
split with the girls in one group and the boys in another. After
planning time, each group was to put on their play for the class.
The girls worked hard and came up with a nice little skit within
fifteen minutes. The boys clowned around and when the time was up
were disappointed that not much had been accomplished. What was
beneficial to both groups was the after discussion of what had
happened in each group that affected the results.

One important thing to remember when you are doing "group
readiness" activities in your class is that the process is as
important as the outcome. Frequently, the results are discussed
but not the way they came about. Even young children are old enough
to learn that how they function in a group affects the outcome, even
though it may not be as important to them now as it will be in later
years. They are able to take a step back from the end result to see
what happened along the way. This process can also be used as a
problem solving technique. One third grade teacher put this to
good use when there was a problem at recess. One of the children
had punched another, who had come crying to the teacher. She asked
everyone in the class to draw a picture of what had happened at
recess. Most of the children drew a picture of two children, one
hitting the other. She then asked them to put themselves into the
picture, to draw in where they were and what they were doing. This
led to a discussion of what some of the other children might have
done to help avert the crisis. Some discovered they could have done

nothing, and others saw that they might have helped. The process of working this through was the beginning of group awareness for most of the children in the class.

These ways of helping children develop responsible, constructive ways of relating to each other are important. While most primary grade students frequently do not develop strong group alliances, there is often group contagion - one child begins a behavior which spreads like honey (or manure) throughout the group. Helping the children learn how to become aware when this is happening may be of assistance in using this phenomenon constructively or in controlling it.

Beginning Management Skills

By the time children are in second and third grade, they are usually ready to assume some responsibility for classroom management. Beginning with some fun activity, such as planning a party, you can teach your students to make decisions, to help make some rules and to analyze and understand the consequences of their behavior. By the third grade, many children are members of natural friendship groups, and it is important for them to learn some of the things that happen in groups and to take responsibility for making constructive contributions. I wonder how many of you give your students a chance to understand what is happening that makes them happy or unhappy in the groups of which they are a member? How often do you give the pupils an opportunity to discuss some of the things they can do to effect change?

There are many ways that a teacher can use groups to help with this learning. One is to give part of the classroom management over to the children, with the teacher acting primarily as consultant. Student controlled decisions might be as simple as deciding how to line up for recess, how to assign seats, or how to distribute the various "jobs" that need to be done. Whatever the question, a committee of students can be formed to discuss the issue and make a report back to the class. Then the class can decide, by vote or consensus, what they want to do about the situation. At first, when you give third graders a task, it may not work out very well. Because they have not had experience in this form of management, they will make many mistakes. They may come up with some wild ideas about how to handle recess or job assignments, for instance. What is hardest for the teacher, yet very important, is to let the children REALLY make the decision. The teacher may point out options and possible repercussions, but if at all possible, the final decision should belong to the children. This is a time when you can teach the students to use Step Five of the problem solving process. "What do we do if it does not work? How long should our trial period be?" To allow the children to make the decision and learn from the results is of value indeed.

Sometimes, some of the craziest, most "far out" ideas that children suggest turn out to work beautifully, and I am rather embarrassed that I did not think of them first. Other times they are disastrous, and I have an opportunity to help the children pick themselves up, dust themselves off and go on to try again. How rewarding it is to see a group of children who have made a plan that did not work move beyond blaming each other to accepting some responsibility for the decision and developing another plan to try. These are the years when children are most creative and most flexible.   If we allow them to flex their creative muscles, they will continue to develop.   Our encouragement and faith that they can complete a task is of prime importance to these budding young group participants.

Chapter Six

CLASSROOM GROUPS OF MIDDLE-ELEMENTARY CHILDREN
(FOURTH THROUGH SIXTH GRADES)

Children in the fourth through sixth grades are beginning to have close, natural affinities to one another in groups. Many sociologists call this stage of life the "gang age". During these years young people have a powerful sense of identity with one another as well as a strong skill orientation as a way of being acceptable in their peer group. For this reason every teacher in a classroom works with a group every day, whether she likes it or not. In addition, because groups are forceful at this age, she has the possibility of harnessing that group strength to encourage learning.

For most children, these years are a period of rapid mastery of a variety of skills which often improve self-concept. Athletic prowess, relationship skills and academic achievement are all very important ways children increase their feelings of self-worth. Other children do not learn as rapidly. Some do not learn because they lack confidence in their ability to master something new. Still others may be physically, mentally or emotionally unable to learn even such basic skills as reading and writing. In addition, how every child is treated by and communicates with his peers is directly linked not only to his relationship ability but also to his skill achievement. It is hard for eleven year olds to like the boy who struck out in the last of the ninth inning. Such negative group pressure is difficult to take and leads many youngsters to turn on themselves. It is in the merging of these self-concept issues with learning needs and peer pressure that groups can be helpful or destructive.

I talked with a fourth grade teacher who said that she really loved children who were nine and ten and that she had had some very positive experiences in teaching fourth grade. She added that she had also had some of her most difficult teaching years at the fourth grade level. I asked her to share some of the differences between her good years and bad years. In the good years she had had what she described as a group of children who were usually nice to each other, who responded to her, but more importantly, who related to each other in helping kinds of ways. In every year which she described as being difficult, or even devastating, for her she had had a group of children whom she felt were mean to each other. She said that she could have tolerated their unresponsiveness to her but she could not live with the way they turned on one another.

Each of you, I am sure, has had good years and difficult years as a teacher. My hunch is that how the class functioned as a group had a great deal to do with what you perceived to be a positive or negative experience. One teacher disagreed with me strongly when I made this statement. He said, "I've had my most difficult years when the group was very strongly against me. I like it better when I have a collection of individuals. Then I can make it with at least some of them. But when the group jells and shuts me out, I have a very difficult time."

Whatever kinds of groups exist in your classroom that are easy or difficult for you to work with, there is no doubt that the group is a very powerful influence in grades four, five and six. Knowing this, you may want to learn some of the ways to use group process in the classroom to help with discipline, to facilitate classroom management, to enhance learning, to develop values and to increase social skills. Take a moment to ask yourself if you want to work toward all these goals. Is it your place as a teacher to enhance social functioning? To develop values? Or, do you see your role strictly as helping these young people assimilate certain volumes of knowledge which are needed to go on to the next grade?

Whether you choose it or not, these young people are working on their social skills, and whether you choose it or not, each young person in your class is struggling to find some areas of competence that will make he or she feel more worthy, both individually and in the group.

Classroom Management

It might be helpful to explore a few of the ways that groups can be helpful in a classroom so that you can decide which may be of use to you. I have already mentioned the concept of classroom management. This idea is related to the discussion in a previous chapter about helping children learn to take more responsibility in the classroom. If you are going to be a process-content teacher, grades four through six are the years when you can most effectively help children assume responsibility for themselves and their own learning. Anything they learn during this period about how to be helpful in groups, they will take with them year after year. This knowledge will not be undone or lost. Even if they move back to a more traditional classroom, they will find that most of what they have learned about taking responsibility for themselves will be retained, both individually and collectively.

You have many choices of ways to go about helping the children get involved in classroom management. All of the approaches require spending a fair amount of time on process issues during the first two or three weeks of class. Approximately 25% of that time will be spent in training these young people how to respond to each other in a group and helping them develop ways of working together and with you that will facilitate the learning process.

One fifth grade teacher met with her class the first day of school and put on the board what was most important to her in the year to come. She included the importance of safety, something in it for you, something to contribute, and somebody cares, to try to spark student interest as well as set a positive tone. She then told the students a little about herself and her broad personal goals for the year. Next, she tried to get the students involved by asking each person to do some thinking. Who are you? What do you need from me to help you learn? How can we help each other so this class can be a good place for learning and one where it is fun to be? The first day the students tried to guess what it was the teacher wanted them to say and to say it. This particular fifth grade class had heard how nice the teacher was and very much wanted to please her. When they finally realized that pleasing her meant taking responsibility for themselves, they began to work hard, first in small groups, and then as a whole class, to develop a set of rules that they thought would be necessary for the class members to work cooperatively together. Now, these rules worked for a while, and then one by one each rule had to be reevaluated and changed as the needs of the class changed or as the students learned more about one another. Eventually, many of the rules became class norms. At all times the young people assumed some responsibility for how that class operated.

When the teacher shared this experience with me later in the year, along with her excitement at helping the class take responsibility for itself, she said, "I was reluctant to begin using this approach because I was afraid I would lose control of the class. Yet, I found that I didn't have less control, I had more control. It wasn't me against them, it was all of us together, struggling and working, with me insisting that they stick to the task and facilitating the completion." She makes an important distinction here which deserves some attention. The process teacher controls the process of what goes on. He helps the children make manageable rules and helps them decide what the repercussions should be for breaking the rules. He facilitates the discussion, but the results are not solely his but rather belong to the class as a whole, including the teacher. Because every person in that room, from the teacher to the youngest pupil, has been a part of the decision-making process, each person has some investment in making it work.

I need to add a word of caution here because I have often been misunderstood when I say that the teacher and the students work together to set the ground rules for their learning experience. It is easy for a teacher to set up a class to act out, on the teacher's behalf, against one of the students, and I caution you that to do so is very destructive. There is a big difference between saying to a class, "Something is very wrong here - people are getting hurt. What are we going to do about it?" and saying to that same class, "Class, what do you think we should do with Johnny because he is bad?" The first intervention helps every member of the class assume responsibility for dealing with their own feelings about a particular class member. A good teacher never asks a class to assign discipline or punishment to any of its members. If you are angry with a child, if she has clearly broken the rules, and you want to discipline her, then that is your decision and you should do so. There is a fine line, I realize, between that action and the approach I am suggesting for children taking responsibility for themselves in classroom management. Hopefully, each of you will be able to help the class function in a way that makes sense for both you and your students, without avoiding the times when you must move in as a disciplinarian.

Three Types of Decisions

Some times it helps to clearly spell out what responsibility is yours and what belongs to the class. One teacher who works with sixth graders recently illustrated how three kinds of decisions operate in his classroom. One type of decision is mandatory. These are not discussed with the class. He says, "This is the way it's going to be." This kind of decision may be imposed either by state law or school rules, such as, "You may not smoke in class," or it may be a decision based on classroom behavior which he thinks is absolutely essential, such as, "You can't take things that don't belong to you." "You can't hit anybody." Such decisions, or rules, are rigid, invariable and inflexible. The teacher always metes out swift justice if rules like these are broken.

A second type of decision is what he calls a negotiable decision. He tells his students, "Each of us is going to be a part of this class. I expect you to consider what is important to me, and I will also consider what is important to you." Such decisions are negotiated among class members and between class members and the teacher, with the desires and needs of the class as well as those of the teacher being considered. One example of how this teacher negotiated a decision was in helping the children decide where they were going to go on a field trip. That was clearly a negotiable decision. He wanted to tie in the field trip with the unit the class was studying. He also wanted the children to act responsibly on the trip so he would not have to be a "policeman". After sharing with the class these considerations which were important to him, he asked each student to write down what was important to him or her. Then the class as a whole worked to find a trip everyone would enjoy. A consensus was reached, and a satisfying field trip evolved out of this decision-making process. When he told me about it later, he said, "The field trip was great, but even more fun was working together to make the decision. I really didn't think those kids could ever reach a consensus, and they surprised me when they did."

A third type of decision in his classroom belongs to the young people themselves. He feels that every class member ought to have some decisions that the teacher might assist in making but are really the student's choice. In his class if the children have free time (or what he calls "quiet free time", which means the classroom cannot become a mad house), he believes that time ought to be truly free and that each young person should decide for himself how to use that time, either alone or in small groups. The teacher, then, is available to help with the sorting out process. He might go to Charlie and say, "Charlie, I see that you're reading a comic book. Why? Do comic books mean something special to you?" Charlie, then, either says, "Nah, it's not important -- I didn't have anything else to do. I'm bored." (in which case the teacher can help him find something to do), or Charlie might say, "Yeah, this is really an exciting story." Allowing children at the fourth, fifth and sixth grade levels some decisions which are theirs, with the teacher acting as a consultant in discovering options, helps them to become more mature and responsible.

Now, there is a problem in using a teacher as a consultant. Many children see a question by a teacher as a challenge or as a putdown. You will, therefore, have to reeducate your class and reassess yourself if you are going to try this approach so that you and your students will know that a question is a question and a comment is a comment. Otherwise, when you go up to Charlie and say, "Why are you reading that comic book?" he will say, "I'm sorry, Teacher," and put it down, or he will get angry with you. To understand why you are misunderstood you must look to yourself first. Are you really asking a question or do you think he is wasting his time reading a comic book? Then you have to educate your students to differentiate between a question and a challenge. I do a lot of questioning as I teach, but I spend part of the first two weeks of every class in educating my students to hear my questions as questions and being very sure that if I have a comment to make, I make it as a comment and not as a question with a comment implied. This distinction is particularly important at this grade level.

Teaching in Groups

There are many other ways that you can use groups in the classroom. This is a good age to introduce small group projects as a way to enhance learning. For example, if you are working on science experiments in a fifth grade class, are there projects which can be done within small groups? Can children participate in groups depending on their interest in the project or on whom they would like to work with and develop some finished group product? Grouping by the children's interest has a number of beneficial side effects. First of all, when students work together as a group they tend to learn more, if they are not goofing off. If they really settle down to business, most students master more than if they work independently. Second, it is advantageous for people who are bright, who can conceptualize very easily, and who go to work very fast, to have to slow down and participate in the group process. Part of the learning for these students is to develop the ability to listen to people who do not grasp concepts as fast and become increasingly able to assist group process without putting people down.

There is another important dimension to this type of group teaching and that is helping people learn how to reach decisions and to master tasks in groups. As must be very clear by now, my bias is that the role of the school is not only to impart pieces of knowledge but to help each individual develop a style of learning which will work for him when he gets out of school. I know of few positions or jobs where group task performance is not anticipated and expected. Even workers in a factory assembly line participate in group decision-making at their union meetings, deciding on shift schedules and in many other ways. Fourth through sixth grade is a prime beginning learning time for this mastery.

Group learning can enhance both cognitive learning and the students' ability to cooperate in a group. Your goal in group teaching, then, is to work on both of these issues simultaneously. Thus, the evaluation you do of a group ought to include not only the final product but also how the members work together.

One teacher tried group learning for the first time with her fifth grade class and found it very disappointing. She said the children fooled around all day long, and then one girl went home that night and worked out the solution with her father. The next day the group presented it as a group-completed product. I certainly agree that kind of learning is not particularly helpful to anybody (except, perhaps, the girl's father). But I think the whole situation might have been averted had the teacher sat down with that group and explained not only the task but how group members were expected to do it together. Also, while the children were working together, she should have had ongoing contact with the group, not only to assist their progress toward task completion but to aid the group process. She might have asked group members several questions. How are you working together? How far along are you on the project? Who is doing what in the group? Who is taking leadership? Is everybody contributing? These questions help the children keep focused on the dual purpose of their group project.

You can also support group process learning by your use of grades. It is feasible to grade both components of group learning by evaluating not only the children's finished product and what they have learned, but also how they went about their task. Every member of the group should get the same grade, since each member bears equal responsibility. Using this approach, it might happen that some small group with a magnificent finished product would get a lower grade than another group whose finished product was not so special because the second group worked well and cooperatively together. Such emphasis on process strongly encourages groups of children to make the effort to work well together.

Class Members as Problem Solvers

If you have allowed your class members to set some of their own rules and to participate in decision-making, you can also involve them in the problem solving process when something goes wrong. Now the "something goes wrong" might be problems outside at recess or in the lunchroom as well as something that is happening within the classroom. I have found there are three conditions that must be met for classes to participate in effective problem solving. First, the focus must be on what happened and not on assessing guilt or blame. That is crucial because otherwise these young people will simply turn on each other and say "Nancy did it." They will try to blame each other, and that is not very helpful. But if your focus is on what happened, then you have a chance of educating these children how to problem solve in constructive ways.

The second condition that must be met is that there always has to be some plan of action agreed upon to make things better. Particularly in sixth grade, it is easy just to have a gripe session - "This isn't fair, that isn't fair." Problem solving requires some plan of action which the children develop and which they have a part in implementing.

A third condition is that the children as a group do not set punishments for one another. I mentioned that as a teacher, even though I am very strict, I punish very rarely because I do not see that as an effective part of the problem solving process. If, however, you find that somebody is behaving in a way which compels you to act, then the choice of action belongs to the teacher and not to the students. If you ever ask a class to mete out punishment against a student in the class you will usually find two things happening. One, is that the children will be harder on that person than you would be, which may, or may not, be appropriate. Two, is that the class as a whole may get thrown "up for grabs" because the children are worried. "If we punish one child, then who is going to be next?   What will the group do to me if I misbehave?" Particularly at this grade level, any disciplining ought to come from the teacher or principal and not from the children themselves.

Even while using the problem solving process, the children may come up against a person whom they cannot handle. They may need help from you to deal with that person, and that is legitimate. You must then follow through with that student. I would not make a decision, however, that any one person need be singled out for special   attention, negative or otherwise, until I had a clear assessment from the class as to what the problem was and how it came about, and the class as a whole had tried to do something about it.

Averting Scapegoating

Back in Chapter 2, I mentioned that I thought that everything that went on in the class was in some way allowed to continue at least with the tacit approval of most of the people in the class. If nothing else, no one did anything to stop it. If the behavior of an individual is intolerable, and students do not like it, they may try to stop it, or they may come to you and ask you to do something about it.   Sometimes they are afraid of retaliation outside of class if they complain directly to the student, particularly if he is a bully. You may need to intervene, even knowing that the bully may feel isolated and alone and is pretending he does not care. Or, the disruptive student may be acting out the anger of many of the children in the class, so they ask you to intervene rather than stopping it themselves. Whatever the roots, any misbehavior in a classroom is in some way connected to the group process.

An interesting example of how this works occurred in a fifth grade classroom a few months back. A class had spent much of the day making a mural which extended the whole length of the room. The mural was a pictorial story of what the students had been working on in class for the last two months, and they were getting it ready for Parents' Night. The children were very excited. All of a sudden, seemingly without warning, one girl picked up a black crayon, and, walking along the mural drew a line through everybody's work. The class was absolutely furious, and the teacher was frustrated and angry because all of his hard work seemed to have been destroyed. Fortunately, the bell was ready to ring for recess, and the teacher was able to say to the class, "We're going to have to decide what to do about the mural and what to do about Ellen, but let's have a good recess, and then we can talk about it when we come back." He also was smart enough to ask Ellen to run an errand during recess so that she would not get clobbered.

After recess the teacher sat down and said, "Okay, class, what happened?" Immediately there was a tirade against Ellen. The teacher by this time had calmed down, and understanding that Ellen frequently reflected the mood of the class, said, "Let's see if we can explore together what happened right before Ellen drew the black line and figure out what things led up to this disaster."

As the children began to shift their focus from their anger at Ellen to what had happened, the class discovered a number of precipitating events that had led up to her destructive behavior. First of all, the teacher had come to class in a bad mood, and though he had tried to cover it up, the children had sensed it and had thought that he was angry at them. This particular discovery was painful for the teacher because even though he knew he had been upset when he came to class, he thought he had done a good job of hiding it. But the teacher was not completely to blame, nor was anybody else - not even Ellen. As they went on to explore what had happened, the children remembered that the teacher had said something that had been interpreted as a snide, cutting remark to a very sensitive boy. He had, in turn, knocked the books off another boy's table, who had, in turn, stolen Ellen's pencil. It was at that point that Ellen had picked up the crayon, and (having felt shut out by the others all day) expressed her anger by drawing the black crayon mark. What was interesting was that as the class began to share more and more about what had happened, each person began to own his or her piece of responsibility. One girl said, "I saw that Ellen was getting mad. Maybe I could have said something to her." and the students became increasingly enthusiastic and excited about discovering what had gone wrong.

When that part of the discussion was over, the teacher moved on. "Okay, he said, "What are we going to do about it? Parents' Night is tomorrow." Ellen volunteered to stay after school and see if she could do something to fix the black line she had drawn. With that, two other girls suggested, "Hey, we could make mountains!" I am sure the mural was one of the most interesting the parents had ever seen, because in the background of the class's pictorial description of what they had been studying, was a group of mountains with a black line through them. The children, instead of ending up feeling furious with themselves and each other, came to Parents' Night with a sense of pride.

At this age level, as you know, there are a variety of different kinds of symptoms which unhappy children exhibit. This is a prime time for stealing, lying and being mean to one another. Most of this behavior has two parts to it. One is the child himself, who feels uncomfortable, unlovable, unable to achieve in the way he would like, or who lives in a community where learning antisocial behavior aids in survival. The other is the group as a system -- how group members feel about themselves and how the group treats others. In either event, helping the class as a whole also will help each individual feel better about himself. It is important that teachers learn how to help children keep from being scapegoated or picked on in class.

Sometimes you have the advantage of being able to anticipate problems and work with a class before a crisis occurs. One fourth grade teacher came to me and said, "I don't know what to do. I'm in a White, middle class community, and I know we're going to get a nine year old Puerto Rican boy who has come from a very deprived home. He's going to be the foster child of someone in our community but he's never, ever, had a good experience in school. I'm really worried that he's going to be very different and that the other children will scapegoat him." As we discussed what she could do we realized that perhaps the best thing she could do was to capitalize on his difference from the other children. What did he, as a Puerto Rican, have that those other children did not have? What might they want from him? What were they willing to give in return?

Fortunately, the teacher had a day and a half with her class before the boy came. She was able to talk with them about him, to share a little of his background and to ask the children to get together in small groups and figure out what things they would like to learn from him. One group said, "We bet he knows Spanish. We'd like to learn some Spanish." Another group said, "We've never lived anywhere but this town. We'd like to know what it's like to grow up someplace else." Then they moved to discussing how the Puerto Rican boy might feel uneasy and what they could do to help him be more comfortable. By the time the boy got there, the class had mastered two things. First of all, they had something they wanted from him that he was capable of giving. Second, they had a plan of action for how they could help him feel included in the class.

The teacher was amazed at how able the class was to take the problem she presented to them, to run with it, to make a plan of action and to succeed with it. And, this was a real success story. That boy made a beautiful adjustment in the fourth grade. His brother, who was a sixth grader, went into a class which was not prepared for him and had a much more difficult time, which ended by his being badly scapegoated. It is hard to know, of course, how much can be attributed to lack of preparation of the class and how much to the differences in the two boys or to the differences between the fourth and sixth grade classes. I cannot help but wonder, though, if that sixth grade class had been excited about their new classmate coming and had done some preparation, whether the older boy, too, might have been able to make an easier adjustment.

Unscapegoating

That kind of advance warning is not typical in most schools, and frequently a teacher has to make a decision about what to do after the scapegoating has already begun. You may have somebody in your class who is very different, who is a natural butt of jokes and whom the other children pick on. Such scapegoating is usually hard for a teacher to deal with, but it is worth a try. As a first step, the teacher must look at herself and her feelings about that young person. Next, the teacher should check the reality issues. Often there _are_ things about that person that are repulsive, that "turn off" the teacher and the children and make him or her hard to like.

Sometimes the teacher can work directly with the child to try to get rid of some of the factors that are so repelling. One teacher had a pupil who came to school dirty, who seemed to never wash. He was terribly unhappy that he was not able to make any friends. She finally took him aside and said, "You know, I think one of the reasons the kids are picking on you is because it's not terribly pleasant to be close to you when you smell bad. Maybe if you could do something about that it would be helpful." Because the teacher was really concerned about this child, he heard this as caring and not as a putdown. The boy told the teacher that he wanted to be like the other kids but several things worked against him. First of all, in the rooming house where he lived there was only one bathroom down the hall, and in the morning before school, there were so many people crowded into it that he never had a chance to take a shower. Besides, he said, he really did not like to shower anyway. Nobody else where he lived cared about physical appearance and people would think he was queer if he was always clean and neat.

Accepting the validity of this concern, the teacher worked out an arrangement with the boy whereby he would keep a clean shirt at school. He would be allowed to come into school early to go into the washroom and make himself presentable with the help of soap and water. This arrangement was not for the teacher's benefit but so the boy would feel better about the way his peers responded to him. What made the difference, what made him excited about the plan is that the teacher built on something _he_ wanted, rather than giving him the message, "You're bad."

Differentiating Home from School. Another important dimension of the above teacher's role is her acceptance of the student's life style at home. Rather than saying to him that the rooming house where he lived was terrible and unhealthy, she said, "Okay, if that's the way it is at home -- if it would feel awkward to take too many showers and be too dressed up at home -- what can you do here to get what you want?" As a teacher, you do not have to evaluate what happens at home. Instead, you can separate that out from what happens in the classroom. And, one of the exciting things about this age is that the young people are very able to make that separation for themselves. I have worked with some youth from extremely deprived communities where the home conditions and expectations were very different from those at school, who had been able to totally separate their experience in school from their life at home and function in very different kinds of ways.

Now, some people may question how helpful such differentiating is for children and adolescents. But my experience is that making this separation is something everyone does all of the time. People operate in different ways in different situations. If you do not insist that the child choose between school and home, he can decide to behave in different ways in each place. If he can successfully do this, he will feel better about school, his home and even himself.

     Building on Commonalities. There are times when you cannot
work individually with a child who is being scapegoated. Maybe a
child is being picked on because she is slightly retarded, because
she is slower than the others, and the children do not want to be
with her. Or, maybe she is physically inept and cannot run as fast
or play ball as well as the others, and nobody wants her on the
team. In such instances, it may pay to take some time in class to
talk with the children about what it is like to be different.
Children at this age tend to scapegoat most often those young
people who remind them of a part of themselves. If somebody is
unable to run fast, the children pick on that person not only
because they might lose the game if they get stuck with him on their
team, which is very real, but also because he represents the piece
of them that is slow or behind or left out.

     One fifth grade teacher had a boy who was being scapegoated
because he stuttered and, of course, the more he was picked on the
worse he stuttered. She discovered that when she was alone with him
and treated him gently his stuttering decreased markedly, but as
soon as the children began to mock him it became worse. Her first
response was to tell the children they were being cruel and to stop
ridiculing him. Later, she tried a different approach, which
turned out to be much more effective, though some of the young
people were very uncomfortable during the process. One afternoon,
the students finished work early, and the teacher and the class had
time to just be together as a group. As they begin to relax, she
asked each person to think of some time when they had felt very left
out of what was going on in a group, when they had felt very
different and that nobody cared about whether they were there or
not. After they all had had a chance to share an experience of
being excluded and how they felt about it, she put on the board some
feelings class members had had when they had been shut out. They
had felt angry, hurt and lonely. Then the teacher moved the
discussion to, "Why do you think people do that to other people?"
The class was amazingly perceptive as they came up with some of the
reasons why people are mean to each other and shut each other out.
When the children became very personally involved in the
discussion, the teacher told them right before the bell rang, "One
of the reasons why I wanted us to think about this together is
because I think sometimes we do that to each other here. We make
people who are different feel left out and hurt. I wonder if we
want to continue to do that because now we know how it makes them
feel." Then, she dropped it. She did not bawl them out, she did
not even mention the stutterer's name. The next day the teasing of
that boy lessened dramatically. Those young people were able to
transfer their own feelings about what it was like to be left out to
what was going on in the classroom. Children at this age understand
what other children are dealing with by looking at it through
experiences that they, themselves, have had.

     The above illustration is a very powerful example of how you
can use commonalities to help unscapegoat somebody when your group
is trusting enough and open enough to discuss things with one

another. Again, there are a few guidelines if you are going to use
this method to deal with scapegoating. First, is that you, the
teacher, hopefully, are able to share a piece of yourself. I never,
ever, say to a class, "Tell me about some time when you felt left
out," without my being willing and ready to share that about
myself. Frequently, I share first. I say, "I remember once when
this happened to me, and this is how I felt." You do not have to
share first, but if you do, you are a model for sharing.

A second guideline if you are going to use this approach is to
try to avoid, if you possibly can, protecting the person who is
being scapegoated. The teacher who felt sorry for the boy who
stuttered used to say, "Oh, please don't pick on Billy. Please
don't do this, please don't do that." If you protect a scapegoat
and tell the children not to pick on him, whether you intend it or
not, you communicate two things. One is that you care about that
scapegoat, which is fine. The other is that, indeed, he is very
different, and he needs your protection. This tends to perpetuate
the scapegoating because your protectiveness makes the children
turn on him even more. It may send the hostility underground, but
it does not help his tormentors understand what he is going
through.

A third thing you will have to do if you use this technique is
to make sure it is not a shaming approach. It is very different
saying, "Tell me about when you felt left out yourself," and
saying, "How would you feel if somebody did this to you?" That is
usually heard as an attacking statement, whether you mean it that
way or not. The subtle difference between helping children share
with you where they are coming from and putting them down for being
cruel becomes a very dramatic one.

In this chapter I have tried to describe a variety of ways in
which a teacher can use groups in the classroom to foster learning
and to help children take increasing responsibility for the
classroom milieu. Perhaps the most essential ingredients to help
this come about are the teacher's sensitivity to herself and
willingness to fight for her rights in the classroom, as well as her
readiness to listen to the rights of her children. Understanding
what is happening in groups and freedom to try something new can be
good learning experiences for the teacher and children alike.

Chapter Seven

YOUNG ADOLESCENTS IN THE CLASSROOM

Teaching junior high school young adolescents is perhaps the most exciting, fearsome, challenging, frustrating, fun and anxiety producing job any teacher can have. There is something special, something unique about junior high young people which makes them particularly fun to be with and yet hard to educate. When these youth encounter the complex junior high system a whirlwind of energies is unleashed. Understanding where group process fits into this unusual phenomenon is difficult and essential.

I once heard a lecture given by an eighth grade young man who said, "Junior high school is a zoo, and all who reside within it are animals." My first response was to get somewhat defensive, feeling he was attacking. But as his speech went on and I heard him talk endearingly and also with anger about what it was like to be a student in a junior high school I began to understand what he meant. In many, many ways the junior high school is the captor of those who come inside its walls. Some students see the school as a jailer. Some see it as a warm, protective environment. But the vast majority of young people and teachers with whom I have talked see the junior high system as highly controlling but at the same time extremely unstructured.

One young male teacher once told me, "I think you have to be a little bit crazy to work with junior high kids, and yet I do and I love it." Another teacher who had been teaching for many years responded to the same quality but in a different way. "Kids are very different now than they used to be," she complained. They're beyond me. I don't understand them. The rules we used to have, the old methods of teaching no longer work for me. Some days I even hate coming to school."

Each of these teachers is talking about the same quality in junior high schools, but from very different perspectives. The goal of this chapter is to provide insight into the functioning of junior high school groups and an understanding of how groups are utilized by junior high youth. I hope to indicate some ways that teachers can use groups to maintain classroom order, facilitate learning, and I also hope to give you permission, if you need it, to be a little bit "zooey." While early adolescence is a time of upheaval and frustration for young people and the adults in their lives, it is also a time with rich potential for extremely creative teaching and learning.

The Junior High School System

Consider for a moment some of the dynamics that make junior high schools so unusual. While there are still some schools where seventh and eighth grades are part of the regular elementary program, increasing numbers of young people leave school at the end

of sixth grade and transfer to another, larger school. Whichever
type of school you work in, whether it is a self-contained junior
high school or whether the junior high grades are part of an
elementary school, there are some basic differences, as you well
know, between elementary and junior high programs.

One of the main differences is the aspect of specialization.
Since the sophistication of knowledge of these young people is
greater than it was at the elementary level, and departmental
teachers tend to teach special subjects, usually junior high
students go to a variety of teachers. A teacher may be faced with
four, five, six, seven or even eight different classes of students
who come parading through her room each day. Such large numbers
make it extremely difficult to get to know the students as people.
It makes some of the intense processing that we discussed in the
last chapter virtually impossible, and it challenges the teacher to
find new and creative ways to use groups.

Because the system of departmentalization is in many ways
unstructured and in many ways very structured, the demand on a
junior high teacher to relate to the school as a whole is much
greater than it is on other teachers. When you have eight classes
coming through each day, there is no way you can shut the door and
pretend the rest of the school does not exist. Your own power to
control what happens in your classroom is less than in a self-
contained classroom, (but you probably have more control than you
think). Each group of students who come in are coming from
someplace else, and the external influences upon that forty or
fifty minutes that you have with the class is much greater than if
you had the students all day. For this reason, you must be flexible
and imaginative if you hope to form and use groups for learning
purposes.

Young Adolescents as Students

Perhaps, even more significant are the young people
themselves. Junior high students, as you well know, are an
interesting, frustrating assortment of individuals, pulling
together as a group, pulling apart from adults, and struggling to
find who they are all in one day - or one hour. And because this
special combination of push-pulls becomes so significant and so
crucial to junior high students, a great deal of their energy is
spent trying on new ways of behavior. There are some educators who
believe that the best thing we can teach junior high young people is
about themselves, and that the task of the school is to help
students grow up. Only after that can we begin teaching content
again. I do not agree with this philosophy totally. I do think,
however, that every teacher needs to be aware that an important
part of the life of every junior high student is to find a way to
deal with the push-pulls of relating to peers, testing adults and
finding oneself.

Young junior high students very much need to see themselves as
part of a significant group of people, usually their peers, and
tend to evaluate themselves based on their perception of how these
peers view them, whether that perception is accurate or not. That

perception may be around several things. Being popular is one of
them. Almost every junior high person whom I have ever met would
like to be popular and yet each is afraid, at some level or another,
that he is not likeable enough to be popular. Even a young man or
woman with many friends may have this nagging doubt. One girl who
was extremely well-liked told me, "I know I'm popular, but only
because I'm pretty. If something happened to my looks, people
might not like me anymore." She did not trust her own popularity.
Most students have many self-doubts, and being acceptable to peers
is critical.

One of the ways that young people think they can be acceptable
to their peers is to look like them. A great many young adolescents
go through a period of thinking that there is something terribly
wrong with the way they look. "If only my breasts were larger," one
girl confided, "then I'd be okay." Or, as one young man put it, "I
need to be as tall as the other guys to be accepted." How students
look and feel about themselves becomes all mixed up together and
directly affects the amount of energy they have left to devote to
their studies.

One of the interesting things about the junior high age is
that some young people who are the best learners are those who are
the most insecure about their ability to make friends. This is not
universally true, of course, but some students who get straight
"A's" are not those who are most popular and most acceptable to
their peers. There are some reasons why this is true. Perhaps a
young person who does not have many friends has more time and energy
to study or more need to please adults. Also, many young
adolescents need to push against adults, and a bright student who
is interested in learning and studies hard may feel that he has to
make excuses to his peers for doing so well. The current norms of
that particular group of young people may not support active study.

There are nagging self-doubts which many young people
experience as they are attempting to find an acceptable role for
themselves. These doubts permeate the way young people relate in
junior high school - to their knowledge, to their peers and to
adults. What makes it even more difficult, sometimes, is that the
vast majority of young adolescents do not readily verbalize that
they have self-doubts; they may not even be conscious of some of
those doubts themselves. Young people may act out their growing up
urges by being rowdy, challenging adult authority or picking on
each other. All of these expressive behaviors make teaching in a
junior high school vibrant, alive and frightening. It helps to
know that many young adolescents need to fight adults, and that
need often becomes an end in itself. Even the most understanding
adult will sometimes be backed against a wall by an adolescent
because that is what that young person needs to do at the moment.
Knowing that this can happen to you, and acknowledging that this is
normal for both of you, may be one of the greatest forms of self-
preservation that you will run up against.

Knowing the Teachers
There is another special quality in working with junior high

youth which makes it both exciting and frustrating as a teacher. These children have an uncanny ability to tune in to you as a human being, whether you want them to or not. Most junior high students know their teachers very, very well and seem to have a special talent for zeroing in, not only on the teachers' strengths, but on their weaknesses. One of the essential qualities, therefore, for you to develop as a junior high school teacher is some willingness to be open about yourself and the strength to insist that your students accept you as you are.

Those of you who were taught in the days of "teachers are not supposed to have feelings," will have difficulty working with junior high youth. If you still feel that you are supposed to be in perfect control and never show your weaknesses, you are very likely feeling frustrated with the students of today. When I was in graduate school I was taught that whenever I had a problem with a child I should always focus my attention on the child himself. If I was backed against the wall, I was taught to look at what the child had done. I would talk with him in terms of what he did wrong, or perhaps make excuses for his behavior (maybe he is having problems at home, or ...). It was as if I was looking in from the outside, rather than being a vital, significant part of every interaction. That was much safer and much less satisfying. What has been exciting for me during the years I have worked with these youth, is to see my focus move from the individual student to the relationship which develops between student and teacher. If an adolescent does something which is upsetting to me, I now can see myself as a part of what happened. Instead of telling a student that what he did was bad, I might well say," When you behave this way I cannot teach, and since both of us want you to learn, you are going to have to behave differently." It is not that the teenager is wrong, or that I am wrong, but that the relationship between us is essential and determines the quality of teaching and learning that can go on. This is one of the things which makes teaching in a junior high school particularly important. Whether I choose to or not, I will be known by students. My salvation is in acknowledging that fact and using who I am and my comfort with myself to model openness to change and learning for these transient individuals.

Natural Friendship Groups

Your use of groups in a junior high school is obviously going to be very different from use in elementary schools. You will need to be understanding and accepting of the way the natural peer friendship groups are functioning and learn to push against these young people as a group to behave responsibly. Most junior high classes will not handle classroom management in the same way their younger brothers and sisters might. There are two reasons for this. One is, of course, that if you have the students only once a day for 35 minutes you do not have enough time, or perhaps inclination, to insist that the children take as much responsibility for their class as those who share the same class all day. The students themselves will not have the investment in one class period that they would in a full-day class. Another reason is that since adolescents, particularly young adolescents, need to push against adults, you as a teacher will want to provide

someone for them to push against — to test out some ways to be
deviant that will not hurt them or you.

As a teacher, your modeling of openness and your insistence
that young people accept you, at the same time that you try to
understand and accept them, is important. Since young adolescents
depend a great deal on peer support, much of your interaction
should be with the class as a whole, rather than with one or two
members. One of the ways of life of junior high young people is
trying on different ways of behaving, and the group as a whole has
tremendous power over each individual in determining which
behaviors he will keep. In addition, your class may consist of a
variety of different subgroups, each with its own influence over
its members. You can help by giving an individual student feedback
on how you perceive him. But you can be of the most help by asking
the class as a whole to assume some responsibility for the behavior
of the entire class -- for how they relate to each other, for how
supportive they are. This is one time when if something goes wrong
in the classroom you can sit down and say, "Hey, you can't continue
this behavior. You are going to have to get your act together so we
can get this content mastered."

Negotiating Together

During the junior high years you can do a great deal of
negotiating with your classroom group. One teacher had a strong
negative reaction to the fact that there was so much note passing
going on in her class. She tried everything. Sometimes she grabbed
the notes and read them aloud hoping to embarrass the writer, but
the students just got mad at her and found sneakier ways to pass
notes. She also tried telling the students that absolutely no note
passing would be permitted and that anyone who passed a note would
have to leave the room. Although for a while there was a mass
exodus out of the room, it did not resolve the note passing issue.
What did work for this particular seventh grade class was when the
teacher finally said, "There's alot of note passing going on in
this room. I can understand your desire to keep in touch with each
other - I remember wanting to do that myself. But I also need to be
able to teach, and the note passing is very upsetting to me. Let's
see if we can come up with some solution so that I will not be so
distracted, and you'll have a chance to do something that's
important to you." It took two separate class periods of heated
dialogue for students and teacher to come up with a possible
solution. The discussion went through stages of anger and blaming,
feeling guilty, and then real problem solving. The solution they
suggested which the teacher willingly agreed to try, was that there
would be a five minute break in the middle of class for note passing
and that nobody would pass notes except during that time. They all
agreed on a two week trial period to see how it would work. This
plan worked fairly well and, though it was not universally
successful, things were greatly improved.

A couple of interesting dynamics occurred as a result, however, which fascinated the teacher. One was that once the contract
was made most of the young people stuck to it. She had not
anticipated that degree of cooperation. But even more intriguing

to her was that the number of notes that were passed dwindled
remarkably.   At the end of the two weeks trial she asked the
students, "How come?   Why, when we made this agreement so that you
could pass notes more easily did you end up passing less notes?   I
had anticipated you would pass more."   A couple of the girls in the
class giggled and looked at each other and when the teacher smiled
at them warmly, one of the girls said, "It's no fun if it doesn't
make you mad."   The teacher recognized the need of the students to
sometimes do things just to frustrate adults but she was very glad
that this time it was not at her expense.

Learning Groups

Junior high school is another time when groups can be utilized
very well for learning purposes.   Small subgroups can be
established to study specific areas of student interest.   As I
described in the last chapter, if you wish to use peer support
learning, it is important to recognize that how the young people
work together is almost as important as the finished product.
Therefore, your evaluation ought to consist of both of these
components.

An important dynamic to remember is that since much of the
energy of these young people is spent learning how to relate to each
other, group completion of tasks will take longer than it will
individually.   Group learning contains a major ingredient of
checking each other out.   This is particularly true if you have a
co-ed seventh, eighth or ninth grade task group.   One teacher told
me that when her junior high students worked together in co-ed
groups, about 50% of what transpired was somehow sex related - the
girls were trying to impress the boys, or the boys were trying to
tease the girls, or each was in some way trying out his or her male-
female identity.   My own hunch is that 50% is probably a
conservative estimate.   Junior high school learning groups and
study groups are going to contain a large component of testing and
trying to impress one another.   If you as a teacher see this as
important learning for your students, just as learning English may
be important, then you probably will be able to successfully use
groups for learning purposes.   If, on the other hand, your only goal
is mastery of the content and you get upset every time the group
members clown around with each other, you are apt to become quite
frustrated.   In this case, you may be smart to stick with individual
learning and let the young people work on their relationship skills
elsewhere.   Of course, they will be relating to each other all of
the time, whether you choose to acknowledge it or not.   Many junior
high teachers feel that assisting students with their developmental
task of learning to relate to peers is a very important function of
the school.   Others do not agree.   Whatever you may believe, use of
small groups does provide opportunities for students to work on
content tasks and growth tasks at the same time.

If you are going to use small groups for teaching purposes, as
mentioned in Chapter 3, you will need to spend some time at the
beginning helping these young people develop some constructive
group norms and roles which will facilitate a positive learning
environment.

Confluent Education

There is another way that you can use groups to help young people become personally involved, particularly since junior high school students are so preoccupied with themselves. You can find ways to combine the cognitive and affective learning that is going on in your classes. George Isaac Brown explores this concept of confluent education in his book Human Teaching for Human Learning.* When you want young people to master certain content areas, this method can make the material personally relevant to each student in your class. Combining cognitive with affective learning not only helps with self-development of students, but also leads to increased retention of the academic material. For some reason when young people are learning in ways that are personally relevant for them they not only keep in touch with themselves and what their struggles are, but they retain the cognitive information more than they would if they were just learning facts. Use of small groups in confluent education increases the impact, especially with young adolescents.

One eighth grade teacher who was teaching about the Civil War found his students complaining about the irrelevance of the material. They were bored, they said. Why should they care about what happened so long ago? One day he decided to personalize the learning and did exercises with the students to help each get in touch with what it would be like if their home was invaded. In one exercise, students were allowed to paw through other students' desks and notebooks, and in another, students were told they had to give their lunches to the teacher. Then he declared martial law and said that no one would be allowed to move about, or speak, without explicit permission. After the young people had reacted affectively to such treatment, and had shared their feelings of indignation, anger and helplessness the teacher moved into the content about the Civil War, and helped them see that the outrages they had just sampled themselves happened to people during that period. He related such experiences not only to the treatment of the slaves, but also to the reaction of the South when they were invaded by the North. What was fascinating was that this was not only a very exciting program for the students, but their retention of important facts about the Civil War was over twice as great as that of classes in prior years. Getting the class personally involved in learning through group interaction solidified the knowledge to an extent that the teacher would not have thought possible.

There are other exciting things you can do with junior high school students as a way of helping them retain knowledge and keep in touch with themselves. Any of the Values Clarification

---

*Brown, George Isaac, Human Teaching for Human Learning, New York: The Viking Press, 1971.

material* ought to be directly relevant to junior high young people, and it can be very exciting to help small groups of students in your classroom evaluate current events based on their own life standards and those of their parents. It is important not to be dismayed if their values appear to be different than you would wish. Many young adolescents go through a period of rejecting (or at least appearing to reject) some of the values with which they were raised or that you would like them to have. In addition, discussing with a small group of peers sometimes distorts their perspective. Do not be afraid, however, to push them to explore the beliefs and values they profess to hold and to press them to examine the alternatives, and likely repercussions. The majority of young people, when they really think things through, will make fairly accurate assessments. My experience is that when young people express their allegience to values that seem twisted far out of the realm of reality it is almost always because they have not had a chance to bounce their ideas off one another and the teacher. They have not been challenged to think through the ramifications of those value systems. Our task as educators, whether we are teaching facts or dealing with feelings, is to insist that the young people of today learn how to constructively evaluate the possible outcomes of societal and personal behavior.

Some of you may be thinking, "That's fine for somebody else, but I have to teach music," or "I'm responsible for getting them ready for the Constitution test," or "How can you make grammar personally relevant?" There are, of course, some subjects that cannot be learned confluently, and also some material which must be mastered individually. Small groups are not always appropriate, relevant or helpful. Much of the lack of use of confluent education or small group learning, however, is based not on the inappropriateness but rather insufficient knowledge and interest of teachers in trying new ways of teaching. The old tried and true methods, even though they no longer work very well somehow seem safer, and the tendency is to cling to known entities rather than to try new approaches.

Those of you who are working in junior high schools have many opportunities to take some time to get to know the young people you are trying to teach today. If you do not have time or inclination to try these approaches with all of your classes, how about one of them? Is there one period that some of these ideas might be worth a try? What are the students in that class like? How do they operate together? How are they similar and different from the way you were when you were their age? You can try some new ways of teaching which will be specifically relevant to the interests of these children and that relate to their social as well as educational needs. There is no reason for these two types of needs to be in opposition to each other when they fit so beautifully together. It

---

* Additional ideas for applications in the classroom of values clarification material can be found in Simon, Sidney B., Leland W. Howe, and Howard Kirschenbaum, Values Clarification, New York: Hart Publishing Company, 1972.

is this flexibility, this excitement about trying new things that makes it tolerable, and sometimes even desirable, to be a teacher in junior high school.

Chapter Eight

ADOLESCENTS IN THE HIGH SCHOOL CLASSROOM

I walked through a large urban high school the other day and
several qualities struck me as being fairly typical of most
schools. This school was large, barn-like and very quiet, until a
bell rang, when all at once it came alive with noise, locker-
banging, jostling, laughing, good-natured kidding and yelling.
Almost every possible form of human interaction took place in the
halls during that seven minute break. Then all of a sudden the bell
rang again, and I was alone. The starkness and the solitude touched
me deeply, for it had been a long time since I had felt so involved
amidst so many people and so much noise and so very alone at the
same time. The dramatic change that takes place in a high school
when the bell rings makes understanding and utilization of group
dynamics particularly important. I encourage you to go back
through the chapters on work with classroom groups at other age
levels, for much of that material can be used successfully with
high school students. There are some factors, however, which are
uniquely relevant to high school youth. Most high schools are
large, sometimes huge, bureaucratic structures in which the
classroom can be a port in a storm, or a source of continuing
agitation and isolation. It is fortunate, indeed, that most
adolescents are members of a significant subgroup.

The Complexity of Adolescence

Watching groups of adolescents hang around together, kid each
other and have fun together makes me wistful, and there is a piece
of me that would like to go back to those days when we were
supposedly more carefree. But the other side of me knows that
adolescence is not necessarily a carefree time, and while there is
a tremendous amount of fun that can be had, the search for oneself
which preoccupies the adolescent years can be extremely difficult
and painful. Because adolescents fluctuate so much, and tend to
vacillate in their search for self, how they function in groups
differs greatly from adolescent to adolescent and from day to day
within the same adolescent. The large bureaucracy, the school,
which is supposed to harness these growing, struggling young people
and teach them a wide variety of academic and technical material
has a difficult task indeed.

The life struggles which adolescents have today are much more
complex than they were twenty years ago. When I was growing up the
expectations for behavior were fairly clear. I knew what I was
supposed to do, and it was just a matter of deciding whether or not
I chose to do it. My subgroup and I, as we acted out together and
played together, frequently made choices - to act out against the
existing norms or to follow them. In most communities today what
used to be so clear is now foggy and there is not one "right way" to
do most things. This is true not only in the majority of
communities, but also in the different outlooks that school

personnel have toward educating our young people. I believe that
it is in high schools that there is the most open disagreement about
how young people should be treated. This disagreement includes
everything from dress codes to enforcement of state laws. It is the
responsibility of every faculty to come to some agreement on common
principles around which the school can revolve at the same time
that it protects the uniqueness of each of the teachers.

Every teacher has his own personal orientation and his own
philosophy about what would be helpful to young people. In addition, every adult has some piece of himself which is still a child.
No one ever totally grows up. This is good in many ways for it is
the child piece of every adult that allows clowning around, having
silly fun, becoming irrational at times, and feeling sorry for
oneself. It is also the child piece, however, that gets "hooked" by
some of the behavior of young people.

Adolescents have their own ambivalences. They want to grow up
and become mature adults at the same time that they want to be taken
care of as children. They have a unique ability to display both of
these qualities at the same time which tends to touch the
ambivalence of the teachers with whom they come in contact.

The vast majority of high school teachers are in a depart-
mentalized system trying to teach the same content to a wide variety of young people from many different backgrounds. This is an awe-
inspiring task, especially when you realize that the content may or
may not be of interest to the students.

One teacher who was teaching in high school for her third year
lamented, "Our school has 4,800 students from a multitude of
different backgrounds, different socioeconomic groups, different
cultural groups, different racial groups and different religious
groups - we're a melting pot. People come to our school from
several different communities which are physically isolated from
each other. Most of these young people are bussed to this huge,
stone building, where by some miracle we are supposed to ignore
these differences and teach them something. Sometimes when I open
the door to my classroom and I see this diverse population of
students, some of whom appear to be bright and eager to learn, and
others who look like they could care less, I just want to quietly
shut the door and walk away."

I can understand how that teacher feels. In many ways the
expectations that are put upon high schools as described by this
teacher are impossible to achieve. On the other hand, because the
population is so dissimilar, because things are so mixed up, a
strong teacher who is willing to take a risk for that forty, fifty
or sixty minutes can walk into her classroom, shut the door and say,
"Okay, we've got fifty minutes to have a good learning experience
together. How are we going to do it?" Some teachers can make
learning exciting enough so that most of the pupils can begin to
learn. Eventually these teachers must become reconciled to the
fact that some students will not learn no matter what the teachers
do. One teacher of 15 years experience told me, "I finally have

accepted that there are some children I will never be able to reach." He then looked up and smiled, adding, "But I'm not going to quit trying."

In every school there are different types of learners. Some students will learn in any school, in any situation, from any teacher, regardless of the type of material. Others seem not to learn, in spite of the quality of teaching or amount of individual attention given. Most students are somewhere in the middle. They learn some subjects well but not others, or they respond to one type of teaching but not others, or they seem to need an extra push to help their learning wheels begin to roll. The approaches discussed here are relevant to all types of learners, but work especially well with those who need something extra to become involved academically.

Making Learning Relevant

To attempt to reach as many of your students as possible, you may want to help your class plan the course with you so that each student can try to take something for himself out of the content. This planning session will also help your class construct a foundation for working together to which it can add throughout the course. One teacher tells her class they can build anything into the course that they choose as long as they can convince her that it is going to help them master the material. Last year her basic elementary math class was composed primarily of freshmen who had had difficulty learning math in the past. She had one student who was not responding to her teaching and finally took him aside and asked what he would like to do. "What would be interesting to you? If our mutual goal is to have you pass this course, how can we do it?" She saw him eyeing a nearby calculator as he said, "I don't need to learn math, I can use one of those things." Seeing his interest in the calculator, she gave him exercises to do and let him "play" with it. She then gave him some completed problems in which she had purposely made errors and asked him if he could find the mistakes. Using the calculator to help find errors was fun for him and helped to remove his learning block against math. That particular math class now has a number of calculators which are used by students in many different ways, depending upon their individual learning needs. (The young man who first benefited from this approach is now in charge of the calculators and helps new students learn how to use them.)

Combining Social and Academic Learning

We have a responsibility as teachers to help young people make learning relevant for themselves. Since most adolescents are in groups for the majority of their waking day, in both formal and informal situations, it is a natural approach to use small groups to help students achieve learning goals as well. Many educators include development of social skills as a part of the learning in small groups. One teacher of a freshman home economics class decided to combine social skill teaching, nutrition and accounting all in one unit. She asked each person to write down what would be the dishes of their favorite meal. After each student had done that, she divided them into small groups and asked each group to plan a dinner menu based on a pooling of the dishes that each of them liked. The negotiating that went on was very exciting, and she saw some young people who had appeared "selfish" begin to yield in response to the group. She overheard one boy saying, "I'll give you lemon meringue pie if you'll give me a shrimp cocktail." A bargain was made. After much give-and-take, the small groups of six or eight were finally able to come up with a menu that each group member would enjoy.

The teacher moved from that part of the learning to a class session on nutrition. Were the basic food types covered? What was the nutritional value of the dinner planned? At the end of the unit she found that the retention of the factual information about nutrition was greater than usual. The students reported that they had to remember, after all it was their dinner that they were discussing! One of the students suggested that since half of the class was overweight they figure out how many calories were in each meal. As the small groups undertook this task they found themselves changing the menu somewhat to make it less caloric, and a friendly rivalry began between groups about who had the "best" and least caloric meal. The teacher then sent the students to the store by groups to check out the prices of the foods for their meal. In so doing, the students improved their math skills as they figured the servings needed, number of portions per package and price per person.

The learning in this class, using small groups, took place at many different levels. Class members learned cognitively about nutrition, mathematics and shopping techniques. They learned something about their own food habits, likes and dislikes, and how their eating patterns compared with a well-balanced diet. They also gained skills in relating to one another, negotiating a contract and making a group decision. One small group followed through after the unit was over by preparing and eating their planned dinner, and continued to meet socially as a small group the rest of the school year. Obviously, this plan would work in some schools and not others, but most of you, I am sure, can discover ways to make learning personally relevant for the students whom you teach and find times when group process can be used to effect that task.

Not only can creative teachers make content personally relevant for students, but items of personal significance to students can be turned into effective learning devices. In many schools, for instance, there is a conflict between community and school about expected behavior of students. One inner-urban school found the administration's expectations for conduct of the students clashed with the behavior necessary to survive "in the streets". Trying to merge these two sets of norms was a constant battle for students and faculty alike. One social studies teacher decided to use this controversy as an approach to an upcoming unit on conflict resolution. He divided the class into small groups and asked each group to draw up a list of similarities and differences in the norms within the school and in the broader community. He then asked two of the groups to represent the point of view of the school, two groups to represent the community expectations and two groups to draw up a list of expectations which were the same in both administration and community. He set up negotiating teams to argue out the issues, and come up with some resolution which would be acceptable to both sides. It took several periods for the group which was representing the school to get beyond the sterotyping which developed, but once they did an enthusiastic dialogue took place. By the end of the week they had agreed on certain terms, were closer friends and submitted as a class a list of suggestions to the school.

Working Cooperatively Together

Students in adolescent classes go through a period of testing the teachers and one another. It is important that during this period a teacher understand the dynamics of such testing and not be too upset by it. This is the time when modeling an open, honest but strong approach to dealing with people is most crucial. A teacher can be warm and accepting of her students, without letting them push her around. This mutuality of respect moves from teacher-student to student-student.

Perhaps one of the most difficult tasks that the classroom teacher has is to find some way for the various subcultures and subgroups that reside within that classroom group to work cooperatively together. In one high school where there were a great number of gangs it was extremely difficult for the classroom teacher to get the students to pull together as a group. When she explained how she would like them to break into groups to work on learning tasks together, one frank young man, an active gang member, said, "You're crazy! We can't do that. We can't be seen working with people from a rival group!" The teacher, then, had to make a choice about whether to try to force this issue or to respect their group norms and let them work individually, or just with students from their own social group. Whatever you would do in this situation must be your decision, and would depend upon a number of factors including personal safety, your relationship with the students and the degree of tension within the school. Some teachers can successfully say, "Okay, for this fifty minutes we are going to have a situation in class which differs from the school as a whole. Club lines do not belong here. We are all the same for this period." Sometimes certain teachers can make that statement and help their class function cooperatively together. There are other times, however, when it just does not seem possible for members of rival subgroups to work together in a class. When that is clearly the case, the best the teacher can do is accept that and try to find some other way to make the learning interesting and relevant.

The Two-Way Evaluation Process

Whatever way you undertake utilization of groups in working with adolescents in your classroom, you will find that most young people are able to take some responsibility for evaluating both themselves and teaching approaches. This is particularly true for juniors and seniors.   Many teachers find that this two-way evaluation process is extremely helpful to them in assessing teaching tools, developing new teaching approaches and helping young people build the evaluation component into any learning experience.   You must begin this process in the very first class session when you are planning the course together and setting learning goals with your students.   At that time you can set down guidelines together for how these learning goals can be reached, and the responsibility of each of you to reach them.   It is a natural step, then, to decide how to evaluate each student's progress and which of the goals have been reached.   You may want to allow for suggestions about teaching techniques from the students, as well as set the tone for ongoing evaluation.   Starting the evaluation process at the beginning of the course provides opportunities for teacher and students to exchange continuous feedback so that at the end of the course no one should be surprised by the final evaluation.

The idea for two-way evaluation is outside of the thinking of many educators, but I have found that for students to engage with teachers in a mutual learning process, the evaluation also needs to be jointly done.   A student should be free to say to a teacher, "This is too confusing.   Can you restate it so that I can understand?"   The teacher should be able to say to a student, or group of students, "There are parts of this material which you are not clear about.   You will need to focus more on those areas to be able to handle more complicated concepts."   I am not suggesting that students and teachers are peers in a high school because certainly they are not.   I am saying that the mutual process of teaching and learning can be developed together, and this includes evaluation.

The "Impossible" Class

Every teacher who teaches for very long at some time or another runs up against what he calls an "impossible" class.   This is the class which, for some reason never seems to jell as a group, regardless of what the teacher does.   The teacher may try the best techniques he knows, work actively for positive, constructive peer group norms and spend a good deal of time talking about what is happening and yet all of his efforts seem to be of no avail.   I wish that I had a "magic answer" for those of you who have classes like that, of course I do not.   But in the work I have done with teachers I have noticed two or three things that these impossible classes have in common.   Some are situational in nature.   For some students and teachers, the class right before lunch is the one that is most difficult.   For others, it is the first class after lunch or just before the day is over.   Or, this might be the one class you have with 48 students or with only 11 books to go around.   Sometimes the problem lies at the content level.   If a teacher is not excited about what she is teaching, it is harder to get the class involved in learning.   Or, if the subject matter is not interesting to the majority of the class members, they may have no incentive to work well together.   Sometimes it is the particular combination of students which is a poor mixture, and if you had a choice you would never have them in the same room together.   There may be pupils exhibiting extremes of behavior with nothing in the middle, or a large group of leaders with no followers, or key leaders of several rival groups.

I have had impossible classes from time to time and still feel frustrated when I am unsuccessful in my attempts to make things better. My years of experience have helped me in some ways, but not in others. My expertise does not make me feel any less dismayed at the failure of a class to become a solid group, nor does it necessarily give me the competence to make all classes succeed. My experience with groups has, however, helped me to become reconciled to the fact that sometimes there is not much I can do with a particular class, but that does not mean that I am a failure as a teacher. Rather than sit around and feel badly about it, I have learned to try to get involved in understanding what it is that is holding up the process. What is keeping this class from learning together? That search for understanding helps me cope better with an impossible class, even if I never come up with a plan of action that works.

If the impossible class happens to you very often, you need to seriously take a look at what you are doing to promote or inhibit positive group interaction. What kind of support are you offering to develop constructive group norms? How well are you able to avoid the power struggles which are so prevalent in work with adolescents? When you do get "hooked" how free are you to use the problem solving process described in Chapter 4 to extricate yourself?

With all of the stresses and strains within every adolescent, among adolescents, between youth and adults, and within a huge bureaucracy like a school it is often very difficult for persons within the system to feel significant and valued. If you can help this come about for forty or fifty minutes a day in your classroom, your students' attitudes toward school in general and themselves in particular may be dramatically influenced. It is worth a try.

Chapter Nine

TEACHING ADULTS IN GROUPS

This chapter is designed to help you understand more about how adults learn in groups and some of the ways educators can use groups for teaching enrichment. As with childrens' groups, adult groups need to establish constructive group norms, compatible goals and roles which will help each group accomplish its task. But, to facilitate this process in adult groups differs greatly from doing so in childrens' groups.

Types of Adult Learning Groups

There are a wide variety of adult learning groups with which you may come in contact. Some of you may be teaching in junior colleges, colleges or universities and will want to take a look at how classroom dynamics operate in these schools. Others of you may be leading workshops with adults around specific topic areas. These may be short workshops, perhaps only one or two sessions, or long term groups. Still others of you may be trying to develop a special adult education project. Any committee or action project includes an element of teaching. If you are training adults to become involved in some political action activities, this endeavor also is an educational process, and your knowledge and use of group dynamics will be helpful.

Regardless of the type of adult learning group, there are several dynamics which are quite different from work with groups of children. If you teach adults, you are undoubtedly aware that they are not necessarily more mature nor less competitive nor have less need for personal recognition than children. Usually, however, these competitive and control issues are more subtle in adult groups than they are in groups of children, especially in the early stages of group development. Power and control issues may be acted out through discussion and disagreement about content rather than process issues. In one treatment group of young children, during the second stage of development, some of the members threatened to leave the group or to throw out other members. In a treatment group of adults, the same issues got resolved by discussing, very politely, whether the topic would be of enough interest to the members to continue. It is much easier for adults to get involved in a disagreement about the priorities of the group, or how the learning should take place, than to openly discuss their feelings of competition with one another.

There is another obvious difference in working with adult groups and that is, in many ways the teacher and the students are peers. Everyone in the class is an adult, but one of them is assigned to educate the others. The adult students may or may not be responsive to you as a teacher, and may or may not be interested in what you have to teach. They may or may not decide to become actively involved in their own learning. Adult groups are no less complicated than childrens' groups, though the behavior is frequently more subtle, nor is there any less need to see the group as a system and to help the group develop constructive norms for its members.

The Adult Learner

An interesting phenomenon which frequently happens to adults when they are put into a learning situation is that some of their childlike qualities become more evident. As an adult student, there have been times when I found myself responding to certain teachers in ways that I can describe only as "adolescent". I found myself withdrawing, judging, withholding, complaining and generally developing the same passive-aggressive stance to education which I learned in my childhood. I do not think that I am the only one who tends to respond this way, for I believe that there is stress in learning, particularly when the learning involves some personal risk or commitment. This stress can create a regressive attitude on the part of the student. There is also some very human resistance to being told what to do by an authority figure who is about your age or who may be even younger than you.

In teaching situations which are not personally relevant to the class members, or where there is no challenge or expectation that the adults in the class have to risk themselves, there may be less stress in the learning situation. But there often is at least as much resistance as there would be in a more meaningful class. I once took an adult education literature course, and all of the students sat obediently and listened to lectures about "great books". Though we participated with each other to some degree and group process was certainly evident, the vast majority of our interaction was between student and teacher. This was all right, but each of us felt a loss at not having learned from each other as well, and frequently met after class to continue the discussion. In this particular course, the instructor chose to ignore group process and stick to content issues. This left most of the interaction between him and individual members of the class. He might have decided to use small groups to critique his lectures, or use some other way to get us more involved with each other, but chose not to. Some classes use small groups a great deal to increase the student's investment in learning. When didactic material and group experiences are combined, adult students have an opportunity to decide how they wish to use the information they have gleaned.

Emotionally Laden Content

Some course content is so personally relevant that students are involved from the start. As a student in a course on the developmental needs of children I found I was unable to think about the content without thinking about myself as a parent. I wondered how much I was doing to help my own children meet their needs. Had the course been lecture-style, I would have had to "sit" on these feelings, but because this instructor utilized group discussion a great deal, I was able to express the feelings which had been aroused by the lecture. Also, because I had a chance to relate my own life experience to the material covered, I remembered much more of the content than I might otherwise have done.

When I lead a workshop on what it takes to create a warm, sensitive, honest learning environment in a classroom, frequently teachers have strong reactions to the content. Some teachers challenge what I am saying, stressing the importance of the attitude of the children rather than the need of the environment to be supportive. Some teachers are judgmental of themselves. "Why didn't I think of that?" "What's wrong with me?" "Am I a good enough teacher?" Other teachers get excited about the flexibility involved and the possibility of trying something new. The combination of self-doubts all of us have and the excitement of discovery is touched off by the content of the workshop and built on by small group discussions.

Another emotionally laden course is the one I teach on work with adolescents. It does not seem to be possible to talk about adolescent dynamics without in some way having my adult students experience the part that remains of their own adolescence - their memories, experiences and feelings, both positive and negative. Putting adult students in touch with the adolescent part of themselves makes the group interaction more powerful, and much more goes on between members than might happen if the content was not personally important. As I present material that touches the very being of the people I am teaching, it is extremely helpful to the learning process to give them an opportunity to talk with each other, to share their ideas, their thoughts, their frustrations and their anger, and to get the support of the group. The awareness that you are not alone with your feelings is very reassuring.

The use of the group for teaching purposes is extremely viable because a wide variety of alternatives come out of the group itself to enrich the material presented. I have discovered that many adults have the ability to take what a lecturer says, internalize it and make it theirs, sharing those parts which are personally relevant. Then, in small groups, they can build on the content, add to it, and make the class very rich indeed. How I pity the teacher of adults who feels that she must have all the answers, rather than allowing many of the answers to come from the class members themselves.

Stimulating Creative Learning

There are some classes where your students do not have the majority of the answers, but there are fewer such classes than you might imagine. In the literature class mentioned earlier, the group of fellow classmates who went for coffee after class found out how much each of us knew about the content. How much more meaningful to me was the story of a "great book" when viewed through the eyes of a fellow student who had been unable to read until he was fifteen. How much it meant to have the historical perspective of a book as told by one of the class members who had lived in the community where the book was written!

I can think of very few topics about which adults would not

have something to contribute to the content as well as to the group process. A responsibility of the teacher of adults is not only to impart knowledge, but to give the students in the class opportunities to contribute to the content. This holds true for many different types of classes.

A friend of mine attended a cooking class which started with the chef presenting information on how to make a special steak sauce. There was a surprise ending to the first class, however, when the chef requested that during the next week at home, each student create an original sauce recipe based on what he or she had just learned about making sauces and come prepared to share it with the class. The chef was not content to let the students just sit back and soak up knowledge. He felt it was important for every person to find ways to use the information presented. In giving them the homework, the chef was saying, "I can give you the tools and guidelines, but within you is the power to make the content yours. You are creative and it is just a matter of lighting your flame."

Maintaining the Balance

I need to add a word of caution here. When adults take a class or attend a workshop, they <u>want</u> something. Most adults do not want to sign up for a workshop, pay money for it, give time to it and then have a leader say, "I don't have anything to give you. You can all learn from one another." In the first place, I do not think that teacher is being honest. If she did not feel she had something to offer, she would not have agreed to teach the workshop. In the second place, anyone who makes an investment in time and energy in a learning situation wants something back. While a valuable part of that is sharing with one another, participants in a learning experience also want something directly from the leader. In adult teaching there is a place for both - a place for teacher-pupil learning and a place for peer learning.

Practice What You Teach

When you are teaching adults how to <u>do</u> something, when the class is a "methods" course, it is very helpful to include a practicum of some kind in the course itself. You would not try to teach tennis by just showing movies. You would get your tennis students out on the court to try things out as they learn. Most people do not try to teach sewing by demonstration alone, but by putting the aspiring seamstresses to work. I feel strongly that you need this approach for other methods classes as well. If I am teaching a group of teachers how to use groups in the classroom, our class itself becomes a practicum for developing that skill. I need to model for the class what I am teaching. At the same time I am saying, "Here's what happens in groups," I need to create situations in the classroom so that it will occur right there and the students can see it, feel it and learn techniques for dealing with it.

Not very long ago I attended an institute on education which was sponsored by a state university. Participants were educators from throughout the United States. One session was on "Ways to Teach Empathy and Listening." The presenter who gave this session was demanding, controlling and insensitive to the needs of the group. As he told us ways to be empathetic and good listeners, he behaved in the opposite way himself. If we asked a question he did not like, he put us down, and when one student made a challenging comment, he said she was stupid. Frankly, it had been a long time since I had seen someone as unempathetic as our teacher on how to teach empathy. Because of this behavior, we all regressed to adolescent-like anger at the teacher. We talked about him, wrote notes about him, and learned very little of what he had to offer because of our tremendously negative response to his approach. I look back on this experience with some regret that I reacted in such a way that I did not learn what I might have at that session. But the reality is that the teacher was as he was, and I reacted the way I did, as did other members of the class, and we all left feeling disappointed and angry.

When Things Go Awry

One of the nice things about teaching adult groups is that if things do begin to go awry, frequently a member of the class can let you know that you are not on the right track. If one of the participants in the session mentioned above had tactfully pointed out to the teacher that we were having trouble staying with him, it might have helped. If a teacher discovers that he is not with the group, he can ask the class for assistance to get back on the same wave length. This may be very hard to do. If I feel a little uneasy about working with a group of people, some of whom are older and more experienced than I, it may be hard for me to say, "Hey group, I'm obviously not where you are. How can we get back together?" It may be even harder to listen to their response. If you can, however, it makes you look like a strong teacher who is able to move with the group. If I am making a fool of myself as a teacher, it is really much easier for a class member to sit back and judge than it is to make a positive, corrective intervention. But I have learned through the years that a member of an adult class has the capacity, in most situations, to make things better if he chooses. He can help the teacher refocus in a way which is nonthreatening to the teacher or the students. When no one attempts to do this, it is usually because there is something in it for the class to let that charade continue.

Games in the Classroom

There are many games which adults play in the classroom. The situation mentioned above includes a game called "Let's All Watch Him Fail." This game is where a group of college students, professionals, or other adults have an unspoken agreement to let the teacher fall on his face and get some kind of pleasure out of seeing it happen. Again, that game cannot go on without both the teacher and students allowing it, but it is played a great deal in most schools.

Another game, similar but at the same time different, is what

Eric Berne* calls "Ain't It Awful." In this game everybody sits back and judges and talks about how terrible things are, and nobody has to do anything to improve the situation. This game occurs not only in adult classes but frequently in high school classes and, certainly, time after time in faculty meetings and other adult gatherings.

Another game which I think is equally destructive is called "I Don't Know Nothin'." When I work with a group of teachers, sometimes someone raises their hand and says, "I'm really dumb because I've only been teaching three years, but what do you think I should do about....?" That is a "set-up" question. If I answer it directly, I am saying, "I do indeed know much more than you - maybe you are dumb." If I do not answer, I am letting the questioner down by not responding. I have learned to try to avoid that double-bind by saying, "I think that it is not going to be easy to answer that question since my viewpoint is different than yours. Let's take a look at it together and see what some of the possible solutions are. I will be glad to share what I know about ways to resolve it, and I expect that you can also share some of your suggestions." I have found that when I approach such a question in this way, the game of "I Don't Know Nothin'" can end very quickly.

Games are played with the consent of the teacher as well as the student, and the above game is often liked by teachers. There is a piece of each of us which feels grandiose - which feels like we really do have answers which others do not have, which feels like we can tell people what to do and be right. There is another piece that says, "I'm not sure that I know anything either." When somebody reaches out to the grandiose piece, it is very easy to support that game even though it is not a constructive way to stimulate self-learning.

I have a personal goal when I work with adult groups which has changed over the years. Initially, though I was genuinely interested in helping adults learn, I think I felt the best about myself when my audience thought I was great. If the students left saying, "Hey, you're a wonderful teacher; I really love studying under you," then I used to feel good about myself. Fortunately, through the years, that pattern has gradually changed, and now I am much more interested in what my adult students feel has happened to them than I am in how they feel about me. I would much rather have one of my students leave a class or seminar saying, "I've really gotten something I want to try," than to have that same person say, "Gee, you're great."

I would like to close this chapter by giving a challenge to those of you who are teaching adults in groups. I would like to give you a push to move beyond some of the teacher-pupil games that so often occur among adults, to another less phony game called "You Can Learn It." Hopefully, this emphasis, not on teaching but on the adult student's learning, will lead to adult education programs

---

*Berne, Eric, M.D., Games People Play, New York: Grove Press, Inc., 1964.

that are widely utilized, creative, and will stimulate and free
adults to continue the learning process throughout life.

Chapter Ten

CLASSROOM GROUPS OF "SPECIAL" CHILDREN

No book on use of groups in schools would be complete without spending some time discussing classrooms of children who are considered "exceptional" or "special". Such labels are really nice ways of saying that there is something wrong with the way certain children function in school, as well as elsewhere. Some of these children have mild enough handicaps that they are able to survive within the mainstream of school. Others are put into a separate , more protective, environment. Special classrooms are established in schools to cope with a wide range of problems - retardation, learning disabilities, emotional disturbances and behavioral disturbances. Even some physically handicapped children are often set aside in special classrooms. Such classrooms may be composed of children with similar disabilities, but sometimes they become a "catch-all" for those children who are having difficulty in regular classes, regardless of the reason for their problems.

This topic is another whole book in itself and it is impossible to adequately cover in one short chapter methods of working with these various groups of special children. Each of the problems listed is unique, and a thorough understanding of the dynamics of the particular handicap is needed before anyone can make realistic therapeutic choices about ways to use groups within a special classroom setting. There are, however, some concepts and questions to be considered by anyone who is planning programs for these young people.

One question to ask is which children really require a special class? Too often I visit a special classroom which has some children who could function adequately in a regular classroom if enough support and help were available for the student and the teacher. Children should not be put in a special class unless it is absolutely necessary. The protected environment is helpful to some students, but it also points out their vast differences from other children and may negatively affect their thoughts about themselves. There are many handicapped children who can, with help, cope with the stress of the regular school program. This includes most deaf children who can "sign", children with mild emotional and behavioral disorders and physically handicapped children who are able to navigate around the building. Including these young people with other children might help them accept their handicap as they learn to cope with their disabilities in a more normal setting than a special classroom. When children with special problems are in regular classrooms it is often helpful to have some ongoing opportunity for them to meet together with other students like themselves to share some of the problems they have encountered which accompany being "different" in a hugh sea of "normal" people. Possible group formats to facilitate this plan are discussed in Chapter 11.

"Special" Children in Classroom Groups

Special education teachers, and other personnel who are working with these young people often overlook the power of groups in these classrooms. There are many ways you can use groups to help children learn, manage their own behavior and gain social skills. To assess where it is best to start with group process teaching, it is important to ask three key questions about your class members. The first is, what is the emotional age of most of the children in the class? In a class of emotionally disturbed children, a twelve year old might well be functioning at a four year old level, and his response to groups would be similar to what it would be if he were four. You would not use a junior high approach with someone operating at this lower age level.

A second important question is, how well can the children conceptualize? Learning how to participate in a group setting requires some degree of ability to understand what is expected of you by the other members, and what the rewards are if you behave in that way. Most educably retarded children are perfectly capable of acquiring that understanding and so are some trainables. But there are some children whose IQ is so low, or whose emotional disturbance is so great, that they are not able to conceptualize what being part of a group is all about. These children need strong one-to-one interventions from the teacher.

A third question is, what is the ability of the children to communicate with one another? A child does not have to be able to see or talk, or hear to communicate, though it certainly helps. I have also seen groups of deaf children who communicate with each other beautifully. But there may be some children who are either so absorbed with themselves, or who have such serious handicaps that they are unable to make themselves understood or to hear what others are saying at any level. These children have difficulty using a traditional group setting. With them you will need to communicate with each one individually rather than through the group as a whole.

One of the things that is marvelous about children is that their communication can be very strong without being verbal. I have seen some very distrubed children, as well as people with insurmountable language barriers, who were able to develop a group spirit and communicate with each other nonverbally. Use of words is not a requirement for communication, in fact, words are often used to avoid communication. When a teacher can permit nonverbal communication to develop in her class and build on this, a cohesiveness can develop that is a pleasure to see.

Most special classrooms develop some group identity even if the teacher does nothing to promote it. In the years that I have been working with retarded children I have found that they rarely discuss group process, but they are keenly aware of what is happening in the class and are able to relate well in a group. Most retarded children are also able to learn in groups. As a matter of fact, some mildly retarded children learn a great deal by teaching others in the class material which they have recently mastered.

One of the hardest aspects of learning for a retardate is retention of knowledge and transmitting to others the information that a child has just learned tends to increase the young "teacher's" memory of that material. Teaching each other in groups can be a strong, viable method of learning in many special classes. Have you tried any ways to let your students teach each other? How did they work?

As I was leading a workshop for teachers of special children, one participant challenged my statement that retarded children can develop a group spirit. "I do all of my teaching on an individual basis," she said, "there is no reason to have a group develop." I explained that groups did form, even though she did not acknowledge them. She disagreed, believing that the students did not care much about one another, nor respect each other's opinions, nor even think about the class as a group.

Two nights later she came into an evening session, smiling from ear to ear. When I asked what was up she said, "Mrs. Johnson, I want you to know that you were right and I was wrong." I asked her what had happened and she went on to say, "My class has had a substitute teacher for a week while I've been attending this workshop. This was the first time I had been absent all year, and today was the first time I had been back in school since the institute started. When I walked into class this morning the mass anger at my being gone was so strong that I could no longer question the power of the group." She went on to explain that she had sat down with her class and told them about some of the things we had been discussing at the workshop, and as handicapped as they were, they were able to communicate not only their anger at her absence but their pleasure at her return. She was quite emotionally touched by this response, and when two children held hands and gave her a joint picture they had made in her absence, she was close to tears. At that point, she made a promise to them to try not to be absent so much, and they agreed to watch out for each other if she had to be gone again. This was a turning point for the teacher and the class, and the rest of the year had much more sharing of responsibility for the class.

Regardless of the nature of the disability which brings students together in a special class, they are able to take some responsibility for what goes on in the classroom. Many teachers underestimate the ability of severely handicapped students to help others. Also, it may be a difficult task to train these students to respond to each other constructively. It appears easier to try to keep most of the interaction between teacher and student. The teacher who communicates in only this way, however, loses some of the potential she has for aiding in the growth of responsibility of the students. For example, if there is a classroom of children who are behaviorally disordered, one of the best sources of control is a positive peer culture. For some reason young people can often take more limit-setting from one another than they can from adults. After you assess the emotional age of these children, and their ability to conceptualize and communicate with each other, you will have some idea of where to start them on the road to more

responsible group behavior. Helping these students develop some
form of group identity is a good place to start. Are there some
activities which would make them a part of a group they are proud
of? Could they each make part of a group picture, or help decorate
the room? Could they write a group song that they could sing
together, or tell stories about groups? Any ways you can think of
to help them feel good about themselves as a group will help build a
supportive peer culture.

After this initial step, assess what responsibility the group
is able to handle in the classroom. Can they see that everyone
hangs up their coats or puts things away at the end of the day? Can
the group take responsibility for calling the attendance? Any
responsibility which the group can take is a starting point for
behavior management. You then move slowly, a step at a time
increasing the amount of responsibility the group is allowed to
take, building on one successful undertaking after another. There
will, of course, be slips back and times when the children do not
want to cooperate in a group. A patient, process oriented teacher
will wait out these periods and at the first sign of readiness on
the part of the class, be ready to move again.

If you are working in a special classroom I urge you to take a
step back from the individuals you teach and do an assessment of the
potential of each for working within a group. See if you can find
some new and creative ways to use groups to facilitate better
classroom discipline, practice learning and teaching one another,
and develop the social skills which many of these children so badly
need.

Relationships with the School

There is one thing that is particularly difficult for the
teacher and pupil in any special class in a school. These children
are called "exceptional" and the majority of the students in the
school see that label the same as being called "bad" or "stupid".
Special education teachers need to find ways to help their students
accept their differences and, at the same time, help them move into
the mainstream of the school. Both tasks can be approached from two
levels. Some teachers try to help more normal children have
contact with the "special" children so the latter will become less
frightening. One special education class which had been teased
mercilessly by some of the other children gained recognition and
status by showing a lunchtime movie, passing out popcorn they had
made and inviting students from other classes to join them. As the
movie goers got to know the special education class members they
began to see them as real people instead of "freaks". At this
point, as might be expected, the teasing lessened remarkably.

Even if the school environment is supportive, these children
may feel something is terribly wrong with them becuase they are
different. The teacher needs to help them view their handicaps in
perspective. Some teachers help their students face some reality
questions. In what ways am I different from the other children in
the school? In what ways am I the same? Some of the similarities
might be in the way they look, what they wear, that they, too, have

parents, that they also have feelings and a multitude of other similarities. There are also some important ways that they are different from most of their peers, which they need to accept and understand. It is a mistake to emphasize one side of the coin and ignore the other. As special children learn to accept their similarities and differences they will be freer to move ahead to cognitive learning.

This dynamic of moving from preoccupation with self to learning cognitive material is particularly relevant for children with behavioral disorders or who are otherwise emotionally disturbed, because these differences are not necessarily permanent handicaps. The children, themselves, have some choice about remaining the way they are or moving to a different style of learning and relating. When children are permanently physically handicapped, organically retarded, or have some other irreversible physiological disorder, the focus may be more on acceptance of the handicap and learning to grow in spite of it, rather than trying to move beyond it. Even permanently disabled children are able to learn at a better rate than their current functioning may indicate. One of the ways to set a tone for that kind of learning is to establish a classroom group climate of acceptance of one another and insist that each person in the class do as much as they are able to help create a good learning environment.

Teachers Who Care

There is an essential quality that any teacher who works with these children must have, as I am sure you are well aware. In these classes, more than any other, it is very important that the teacher be in touch with her own affective response to the behavior that is expressed in her class. A large part of the teaching of groups of special children is pushing the students beyond what they think they can do, challenging them to move ever forward, accepting their regressions, and using the group members to help each other in their search for knowledge. In order to do this the teacher must not pity but empathize. Above all, she must be in tune enough with her expectations so that the ones she makes on her students are realistic.

After she is sure that her expectations are not based on her own needs, but on her assessment of the capabilities of the children, she should allow no excuses for lack of performance. Once it has been demonstrated that a student is able to behave or function at a certain level, she should expect the student to continue to perform there. It is very easy for the teacher who feels sorry for a child to make excuses for his poor performance. It is natural for empathy and caring to replace, rather than supplement, behavioral expectations. It is important that you not allow this to happen. One of your best sources of protection from that trap is the children themselves. They can and will let you know when you give up, when you make excuses for them or when you pity them. If you, as a teacher, will listen to the response of your group you will be aware, sometimes with discomfort, of how they perceive your interventions. It should give you some clues about the next step to take in developing a cohesive learning

group. In one class of physically handicapped children the teacher
was amazingly able to push the children to perform at their best.
But one girl had been absent because of her fifth operation that
year. When she returned to class she looked wan and pale. The
teacher found herself pitying the girl, and began to make excuses
for her lack of performance. After a day and a half of this, the
girl looked her in the eye and asked, "Why aren't you yelling at me
anymore? Don't you care if I don't learn?" This girl missed the
caring that the yelling had represented.

Teachers who choose to work with these children are of a very
special breed. They must be able to see a great deal of human
suffering and respond warmly to it, without becoming so personally
involved that they are unable to maintain their own equilibrium.
Some teachers shoulder more of the responsibility for their
children than they need to. In that event, the caring becomes overprotective. A special education teacher must not hesitate to ask
her students to share the responsibility and caring with her. Most
of them can.

Chapter Eleven

GROUPS TO HELP CHILDREN COPE

In every school there are some children who have difficulty adjusting to the system. The first several chapters of this book have been written for those who want to try to maximize the adjustment potential of children, and create a positive learning environment. Regardless how excellent the school, however, there will always be some children who are unhappy and/or exhibit behavior that makes school personnel unhappy with them. Usually these two come together, and it is rare to meet a child who is causing problems in a school who is really happy within the system. Most schools have counselors, psychologists or social workers available to help some of these young people adjust a little better, and/or to help teachers understand their behavior. This chapter provides some ideas for those of you who are in helping positions to establish and manage groups of these children. Some of you may also want to establish teachers' groups to give insights into behavior of these children, and teach coping mechanisms. Chapter 9 contains some pointers about these groups, and many of the suggestions that follow will be relevant to adult as well as youth groups.

There are many different types of groups which can benefit a young person who hurts. Which of these groups would be most appropriate for a particular child you wish to help depends on your interests and skills as a worker, as well as the specific needs of the child or adolescent. Each of these groups can take place at any school grade level though, of course, the type of group you lead in each category will vary greatly by age and interest of the participants.

Groups which have a primary purpose of helping children adjust to school will usually have other goals as well. In fact, some of the secondary goals (i.e., skill training, task completion) usually have inherent value. Also, many groups with a primary focus on other aspects of learning (tutoring, school activities, clubs, etc.) can be developed to include a secondary goal of adjustment facilitation. The groups which appear to be most feasible, and successful, in the majority of schools are those which include treatment with some other goal.

Treatment? In Our School?

There are some ethical issues which are often raised about offering treatment groups within a school setting. There is honest questioning about whether the role of the school includes a treatment component. Advocates of one side of the controversy state that the mental health of every pupil is just as important, and just as much a part of the charge of the school, as teaching reading and writing. Other educators feel diametrically opposite. They say that "automatically" including treatment in the school curriculum is an infringement upon individual rights. They feel that education of school children should be restricted to academic areas with other interventions coming from home or church. There are a wide variety of opinions in between these two extremes, of course, all of which have some merit. Since there are few Federal laws governing this issue, most decisions are made at the state or school district level. Many districts ascribe to the first point of view and children are routinely referred for counseling if they are in temporary or long standing difficulty. In these districts, treatment is a part of the regular school program. Schools in other districts only make referrals of children who have serious disturbances who are then sent to see the school counselor, psychologist or social worker. These districts require written permission from parents prior to any major therapeutic intervention. Still other schools ask pupil personnel representatives to assess difficulties and refer all adjustment problems to facilities outside of the school.

Whatever the point of view of your district, it is important that any diagnostic or treatment services which are offered be a natural part of the school. Diagnostic testing can take place with the same attitude that one tests for academic progress. To help avoid unnecessary labelling of children as sick or disturbed, which may have lasting negative effects, it is helpful if most mental health services in your school are a regular part of the program. The schools which seem to combine these services the best are those where each member of the pupil personnel team is an inherent part of the staff. Each is seen regularly around the school, helps in crisis intervention with children and teachers, and is known by the students as someone to whom they can turn for a variety of services, from sharing the excitement of getting an "A" to crying over the loss of a boy friend. There are some districts which invite representatives from outside agencies to lead groups within the schools. Some of these programs work very well if the outsiders are familiar with, and accepting of, the school goals and operation. If there is conflict between the agency worker's goals and the school's goals, the children in the group have a difficult time adapting to either. Within this broad framework, there are specific types of groups which you can consider which may help children adjust more comfortably. Many of the groups discussed below are not treatment groups, but it is hoped that any group which operates within a school is in some way therapeutic - serves to preserve health.

There are at least five major categories of therapeutic groups which are possible to form, or utilize, within a school: 1) educational groups with a therapeutic or treatment component; 2) task groups, with a focus which includes helping unhappy children accomplish something to be proud of; 3) groups designed to modify behavior; 4) informal discussion groups where young people can meet to talk about things that are important to them about school, social problems, themselves and other relevant issues; and 5) what are commonly known as treatment groups, which may be of many different types.

Educational Groups

Educational groups may be set up with the dual purpose of teaching cognitive material and at the same time helping children feel better about themselves within a school. These groups exist in a variety of forms. The most obvious are tutoring and speech therapy groups. These are widely used in some schools to improve basic skills, impart corrective experiences and foster self-esteem. Typically, tutoring is on a one-to-one basis, but many schools have discovered that small tutoring groups can be more productive and make learning more fun than individual instruction as children enjoy and learn from each other as well as the teacher.

Another type of educational group, which is less widely used, though equally valuable, is a group where students with behavior problems are brought together to teach younger children. This "learn by teaching others" approach not only helps them gain important skills, but helps them settle down by giving them a task to accomplish which has a good chance of success. Two fifth graders, for instance, were active, smart alecky and had a great deal of difficulty sitting still in class. The teacher asked them to go every day for a week to a kindergarten class to teach a group of five year old students how to read a calendar. They were proud to have this assignment, and worked closely with the teacher to select appropriate teaching material which would be of interest to their young charges. The teacher was surprised at the seriousness with which the two boys took on this new important job responsibility and the resultant more mature behavior which they exhibited. After the first day of teaching, the two boys came back triumphantly and reported on their experience. One boy said, "Boy, are they little! The kids were lots of fun, and they liked the lesson, but they sure had trouble sitting still!" This insight for the fifth graders did more to reduce their own restlessness than any method she had tried. There is nothing that heightens one's self-esteem more than being important to somebody, and no better way to evaluate your behavior than to see it displayed by someone else.

Another type of educational group is what I call a "skill" group. This is a group where children are taught basic skills which they have not mastered. One such group was composed of beginning freshman boys who were acting out in biology class. They were being disruptive, taunting the girls and annoying the teacher. One day over lunch, the biology teacher was discussing this when another teacher suggested that these boys were trying to impress the girls. The biology teacher quickly agreed, and added, "If only they could learn some other way!" A gym teacher responded to that comment and suggested an after school group for freshman boys who wanted to learn how to impress girls. He talked with this particular group of boys about the possibility of having a group on "How to pick up a girl and what to do with her when you get her." After a great deal of denial and kidding around, the boys agreed to come to the group. When they saw a teacher respect their legitimate desire to impress girls, they were willing to learn more constructive ways to achieve their goals, and their behavior in biology improved. This group proved much more successful than punishing them for their behavior, or in some other way denying their attempts to be attractive to the opposite sex.

I am sure that you can think of many additional ways to use educational groups to enhance self-esteem and improve adjustment to school. In some districts, this is the most viable, and perhaps the only means permitted for use of groups for other than academic pursuits. This type of group can be formed strictly within the limitations of almost every school, without becoming involved in the treatment-education controversy, or having to get parent permission.

Task Groups

Another type of group which you can utilize within most schools is task groups. These are groups formed with a primary goal of completion of some time limited task. It might be planning a school picnic, putting out a parent newsletter or redecorating the student lounge. A child who is having trouble completing assignments in school, is often very able to complete a nonacademic task, and that ability can lead to a sense of accomplishment which will spill over into classroom performance. When tasks are completed as a group, the individual success feelings are there, as well as a feeling of group satisfaction. Many young people who are part of a successful group feel better about themselves, even if their particular contribution is small. A boy who is a member of a winning football team will feel good about himself, and the victory, even though he might spend most of the game "on the bench". One sixth grader, for instance, was part of a group of girls who were assigned the task of designing the hall bulletin board. Jane was not very artistic, and she had some trouble getting down to work, but with the help of the other girls was able to be of assistance. She carried supplies, ran errands, handed tacks and crayons to the girls and was otherwise helpful. When the group finished, and her name was on the list of workers, she shared in the pride of the project.

Other task groups capitalize on existing programs to help troubled youngsters. Too often we overlook the great possibilities of the orchestra, learning center, drama program or gym activities to help children find a place for themselves. One boy, a junior in high school, was very withdrawn and had no friends. He was referred to the high school counselor by a concerned teacher. His response to the counselor was "I don't care, I don't need any friends. Why don't you leave me alone?" The counselor knew that to insist on treatment would be neither indicated nor helpful. She was not even sure that the boy needed therapy. Here was a loner who was making it, albeit rather unhappily, and who denied any desire for help. Rather than give up entirely, the counselor talked with him about what he did want. If he did not need friends, what did he need? What things in life were satisfying for him? As she began to demonstrate her interest in him, he shared with her his excitement about carpentry. He explained how he had redesigned and rebuilt his room at home, all by himself.

Acknowledging his interest, the counselor later mentioned to

the drama coach that she knew someone who might be able to help with
set design. The drama coach talked with the boy who hesitantly
agreed to try. He found that his particular skill was so much in
demand that some of the other students sought him out to learn how
to construct some of the scenery. Many even volunteered to be part
of the stage crew if he would promise to work with them. As he saw
that this skill was valued by his peers, he gradually gained
confidence in his ability to relate to others. By the time he
graduated, he was much more happy with himself and while he was not
one of the most popular boys in school, he had made some really
close friends.

There are still other ways that task groups can be used to help
children adjust. In one school a group of sixth grade boys became
known as the school "terrors". They harrassed other pupils, teased
girls, hassled teachers and generally were obnoxious. What helped
them was a meeting with the principal where he asked them to share
with him what they were trying to accomplish by their behavior. The
boys openly explained that they needed to be "tough" because they
were the oldest guys in the school. At this point the principal
agreed that that was an acceptable goal and that if they really
wanted to be tough, he wondered if they thought they could
supervise the recess for the K-2 classes. He explained that
several of the young children had been hurt during recess recently
and suggested they might like to help protect them. The first
response from the boys was extremely negative, as you might expect.
"What US! Play with Babies! Never." The principal shrewdly
apologized for asking, saying that he had been mistaken, that he
had thought they were grown up enough to handle the assignment. A
social worker at the meeting responded that he thought the boys
could manage it, and offered to teach the boys some games to play
with the young children. The principal said he thought it was more
than the boys could handle, wherein the fellows accepted the
challenge and agreed to try. The principal cemented the "deal" by
betting the boys a pizza that they could not be tough enough to run
the recess without incident. The social worker sided with the boys
and agreed to work closely with them, and the boys became
increasingly excited about the challenge, as well as working
together to be tough in a different way. "Gee, the whole school
will know how important we are now!" one exclaimed. Needless to
say, the principal lost the bet and three weeks later bought a pizza
for a much improved group of boys.

I am sure that you can think of many other ways that task
groups can be used to foster more appropriate school behavior and
higher self-esteem. As is evident from the examples listed above,
in order for this type of group to be successful the task must be
designed so that it responds to the same need which the deviant
behavior represents. Finding new ways to be tough worked much
better than telling the boys they did not need to be tough at all.

Behavior Modification Groups

Groups which are established to change or modify behavior take
one of several forms, or may combine different approaches. One
type of behavioral group is designed to help children change

specific behavior which is undesireable to teachers, or other school personnel. Another type is one where the children themselves select behaviors which they wish to change, and through the use of games, role plays and other activities learn and try out new behavioral possibilities which may be more satisfying for them than past coping mechanisms. A third type of behavior modifier group, which is undervalued in many schools but which can be very useful, is what I hesitantly call a "bribe" group. A "bribe" group is one where children who are having difficulty maintaining satisfactory classroom behavior are told, "If you can sit still in class this morning, then the last half hour before lunch you can come to group." These groups are mostly fun groups. They have a variety of activities during which the children can have a good time together. It might be held outside, or in the gym, and include games, crafts, stories and anything else which is fun for children of that age. As the group becomes increasingly important to the children, they will behave more appropriately in the classroom so they do not lose the privilege of attendance. Gradually the improved behavior continues without the constant need for group reinforcement.

When I suggest this to teachers, there is often a negative reaction from some of them about the entire approach of rewarding "bad" children for acting nicely when the "good" children have to stay in class. I used to feel that way myself, until one day a group of well behaved fourth graders told me that such groups were important to have around. They said, "We know that we can sit still, but Johnny can't. He needs special help just like we might in math or in something else." We would not hesitate to tutor a child who had trouble with math. We would give him extra time and attention to help him learn and grades and other positive reinforcement for his growth. How different is this type of group?

Discussion Groups

Discussion groups are also multiple in kind. Junior high and high schools often have "rap" groups where youth get together just to talk about what "bugs" them. Other schools have discussion groups where children pick a topic of interest and pursue it, usually with a group leader or facilitator. There are "issue of the day" groups where young people can get together to discuss specific concerns of theirs - anything from politics to grooming. One elementary school has a "Tuesday afternoon group," where every student who has something he wants to discuss, meets with the principal on an informal basis to talk about the school. "It is a chance for me to have contact with the students," the principal said, "and to help these young people understand some of the things I'm up against in running the school. I learn from them, too. The dialogue helps all of us."

Discussion groups are a good beginning place for clinicians who have never facilitated a group before. Young people like to be heard, and often begin to enjoy school more because of this type of group. Obviously, they learn something about the topic under discussion. But even more important, it provides a chance for a captive in a system to be heard (and these children are captives for better or worse). As one regular attender of a "rap" group reported, "You bet I come regularly! I come to school day after day and I'm told where to go, when to go there, what to learn and how to learn it. This is the one time each week when someone listens to what is important to me. I wouldn't miss it!"

Despite their wide versatility and usefulness in schools, there are a couple of cautions to those of you who plan to use discussion groups with young people. In these groups, as in all others, it is important to try to develop constructive group norms. If students speak up and are put down by the leader or others in the group, the entire group is in danger. No one will want to come if it is not safe for everyone. If, however, the group becomes known as one where each student's opinion is respected, and there is no one right answer to the issues discussed, the group has a chance to be highly significant.

Another caution is that this group is not a place to deal with the vendettas and opinions of the group leader. If the children are to really have a chance to be heard, the leader/ facilitator must guide the discussion and not control the content. Still another caution is that the facilitator of such a group must be sure that he does not have a hidden agenda. If a school has a discussion group, there is merit for that group to exist as it is, and there should not be attempts to make it into something else! Too often a group leader organizes what is supposed to be a discussion group but, either consciously or unconsciously, trys to turn it into a treatment experience. When young people begin to discuss an issue, the leader probes for feelings, interprets unconscious material, or evaluates student remarks or behavior. That is not only unfair, it does not work, and the facilitator will be much happier if she sticks to the group purpose and goals.

Each type of group mentioned above has benefits beyond those which are discussed. You can think of many ways that each of these types can play an important part in the atmosphere of your school. If young people enjoy coming to any of these groups, they will, hopefully, enjoy school more in general, cause less difficulty, and have less people angry with them. The better they behave, the more positive feedback they will get and the better they will begin to feel about themselves. This increased self-esteem can mushroom to a generalized feeling of being more worthwhile. There are some young people, however, who need more than any of these groups can provide. They may have such significant disorders that some sort of treatment intervention is indicated, or be unhappy enough to want some help for themselves, or both.

Treatment Groups

Treatment groups are the most controversial of all groups which are possible in schools. As with the other types, there are a large variety of treatment groups, and treatment modalities, which can be used within a school. For the purpose of clarity, I will briefly mention what some of these types are, and then move to an in-depth discussion of one form of group which I believe can be utilized very successfully in most schools.

Intensive psychotherapy groups are those designed to give insight, catharsis and/or other analytic opportunities. Whatever the modality that is utilized (Analytic, Gestalt, Primal, Transactional Analysis, etc.), these are all groups which require a great deal of training, both in specific method and in group dynamics and treatment. Various aspects of each of these modalities can be incorporated in many different group experiences (for instance, some Transactional Analysis techniques are very helpful in task groups), but the majority of these specialized approaches require specific training beyond that attained by most school personnel. Encounter and sensitivity groups, sometimes called enrichment groups, often push hard against peoples defenses and should be used in schools only by experienced trainers, if at all.

One type of therapeutic group which can be utilized effectively with children of almost all ages, without some of the risks inherent in other types of treatment is the "common problem" group. A "common problem" group is one where children of about the same age, who all have identified a similar problem or issue which they feel is important to them (not necessarily the reason for referral), are grouped for a time limited period to work on that one specific problem area. Examples of problems might include trouble making friends, not getting along at school, hassles at home, feeling unhappy alot of the time or many other issues. The commonality of concern brings these young people together very quickly in most cases.

Group Composition. If you are thinking about starting one of these groups, be sure to turn back to Chapter 3's sections on group goals and composition. These groups are made or defeated in many cases before the first group session by the way the group is composed, the compatability of goals and other basic group process issues. There are some specific factors about the composition of these common problem groups which are worth considering. This is one time where homogeneity of problems (as the students see them) and heterogeneous symptoms is extremely important. The heterogeneity of symptoms gives group members a wide variety of behaviors and coping mechanisms to witness and choose from, and the homogeneity of problems gives them something in common around which to relate. Other helpful hints about composition of these groups includes the advantage of single-sexed groups at the sixth through ninth grade levels. This is true unless the goal of the group is better peer relationships, in which case having a co-ed group might be advantageous. For other group purposes, though, it has been found that most students prefer, and work best in, groups of their own sex. As one girl put it, "How can I talk about how I feel about my mother, when I'm trying to get the boy sitting next to me to think I'm great?"

In common problem groups it is also important to avoid extremes of behavior and be sure not to include one child who is very different from the others. It is worth the effort to try to compose these groups to facilitate basic maintenance role functioning, and avoid over-exposure to any one role. A group of all followers and no nurturers can be one long power struggle.

Group Structure. Common problem groups should each have from six to twelve members and meet at least weekly for approximately 40-60 minutes (depending, of course, on the school schedule). These groups work best when they are time limited, meeting anywhere from 8 to 20 weeks, depending upon the issues being discussed and time available. Some groups may choose to meet again for a second semester, with new enlarged goals, which is fine, but it is important to begin your group on a time limited basis. There are several reasons for this. One is that you have a safety valve if things go wrong. It is very difficult to start a group that does not work, and being committed to it for an entire school year can be frustrating for the leader and members. It is also difficult to have a group fail and have to cancel it - both facilitator and members assume some responsibility for why the group did not succeed. Most of these young people have had enough failures in their lives already, you do not need to build in another. But you may run into situations where regardless how well you compose the group, select members and get started, something goes wrong. The group may never get off the ground, never progress beyond the power issues. In these few cases, it is well to discuss with the group what is happening and together decide to end the group rather than continue. Figuring out together what is wrong might help with the treatment process, even if the group dissolves. But having a time limited group might avoid the necessity for such a confrontation, for you can terminate the group at the end of the contract and evaluate it objectively including the positive as well as the negative elements.

A second reason for time limited groups is that it takes a while for a young person to become a significant part of a group and find out if it can be helpful to him. You will find that some children do not use groups successfully. While there is theoretical knowledge about the types of clients who are most likely to fail in groups*, it is hard to predict every circumstance. For this reason, it is good to have an "out" for the young person who is mistakenly put into a group he does not want, or one in which he is destructive. The time limited structure permits this.

Also, the time limited group puts therapeutic pressure on a group to get to work. As a leader or member, if I know I am going to meet in a group all year, I am in no hurry to get started. But if I have only between now and Christmas to find out what is wrong, I had better begin to move. Fortunately, the school calendar provides natural beginnings and endings which make this structure easy to implement.

Forming a Group. A group frequently begins when a worker within a school sees a common need among young people. A counselor may tell a psychologist that there are a number of students who seem really turned off to school. Or a teacher may see a large number of

---

*See Chapter 4 of The Theory and Practice of Group Psychotherapy, by Irving Yalom (New York: Basic Books, 1970)

fourth graders who have trouble making friends. In a large junior high or high school there is almost always need for peer relationship groups. In addition, there are in many large schools a number of young people with only one parent.* Take a moment to think about the youth with whom you work. My hunch is that you will find a number of commonalities around which children can be grouped. In some inner city schools, groups are formed of young people who are somehow "different" from most of the students (racially, culturally or ?) and who need help in adjusting to the "foreign" environment of the school.

After you have discovered some common issues around which groups can be formed, choose one or two that are of particular interest to you. Select some broad goals which you would have for such a group. This is also the time to decide if you would like to work alone or with a co-therapist. Co-therapy can be very helpful in certain types of groups and unnecessary in others. You will have to decide whether you wish to work with someone else, and if there is another staff person with whom you can form a therapeutic alliance.

Once you have ideas for commonalities around which you can build a group, look at the students with whom you already have a relationship. Are there enough students you know with common concerns to begin a group? If not, you may want to let teachers, other school personnel, and students know about the type of group you are starting, and what age level students you can accept. This information should include symptoms which may be indicators of the problem around which you plan to group. One social worker sent out the following notice to students and teachers, "Right after the holidays, I plan to begin a group of sophomore students who are having difficulty relating to their peers. These young people may be loners, bullies, be openly unhappy or have shared their feelings of loneliness with someone else. If you know of someone who might be helped by this group, please let me know. I will talk with them and get back to you about the outcome of our discussion." By explaining not only the type of group, but also what symptoms to watch for, the teachers were much more able to know who to refer.

Screening. After you get the referrals, you should see each student individually. The purpose of this screening interview is for you to begin a relationship with the potential group member and to make a mutual assessment about the appropriateness of the group you have in mind. You will want to discover with him whether his concerns fit the broad goals you have for the group, whether he feels he can contribute to the group, and what he needs from you to make a good adjustment. If you are working with a co-therapist, both of you should be present for this screening interview. Some of the areas you may want to cover include the student's prior group

---

*For further discussion on types of difficulties faced by adolescents, listen to Counseling and Psychotherapy with Adolescents, a series of cassette audio tapes by Joy Johnson, which are distributed by Instructional Dynamics, 450 E. Ohio, Chicago, Illinois, 60611.

experience (especially how he feels he fits into his family and with his peer group); the concerns he has that he would like to work on; some of the things he likes to do for fun; parts of his life which are difficult for him; and his initial reaction to being in the group. (Note: Do not require enthusiasm to decide to put a child or adolescent in a group. A willingness to try is all that is needed for a successful group beginning. Many children, and most adolescents, are rightfully suspicious until they know who is going to be in the group, and no one really knows whether or not this group can help.) The screening interview will, of course, be shorter and different with younger children than with adolescents, but the same basic information can be obtained. The initial interview may last anywhere from 15 minutes to an hour or more.

Be careful during the screening interview not to do treatment. You will, naturally, want to be warm and supportive and help the young people talk about themselves. If, however, you try to work on their problems with them during the first interview rather than reflecting that these are things which are very relevant to discuss in the group, you may be sabotaging your own group without knowing it. If they get the idea that the "real" treatment comes from you, why should they be in a group?

During screening interviews with high school students, you will frequently run up against someone who seems right for the group to you, but who is very hesitant. Help that student share the hesitancy she has with you. What are her fantasies about what might happen? What is she afraid will be the result of being in such a group? Frequently, if she shares her fears with you, and you accept them as legitimate, they will become less frightening to her. Also, you and she might be able to make a contract to help cope with some of her fears. If she is afraid she will tell too much and be embarrassed, you can agree to help her set limits on how much she shares. If she is still ambivalent after she has shared her fears, you can help her make a decision by giving her a chance to change her mind if the group does not meet her expectations. Ask her to try the group for six weeks and tell her that if at the end of that time she wants to leave the group she may, with no questions asked. This has the advantage of giving the student a way out if the group gets too scary, and she is then freer to give it a try. My experience is that in the few cases where a student did want to leave the group after the sixth session, she was right and I was wrong in putting her in that particular group.

Other Important Considerations. After all of the screening interviews are completed, you are ready to begin the group. Most of what was discussed in the chapters on classroom groups is also relevant for treatment groups. Some of the reality factors which are important to success in this type of group are hard to obtain in a school, but it is worth the attempt. The group should have a regularly scheduled time to meet, in a regular meeting room where the group can proceed in privacy and without interruption. Some staff use their offices and crowd the young people into a small space, to insure uninterrupted privacy. Other staff find an available classroom or lounge which is available on a regular

basis. One highly successful group met in the boiler room of an
overcrowded school with the janitor standing guard to see that they
were not disturbed. These space issues are not resolvable in all
schools, but it is important that the administration which asks for
groups is willing to make the investment to provide suitable
meeting space, and to see that children are freed from other
responsibilities so that they can attend regularly.

These specifics on treatment groups are only a start, and the
novice needs additional training before undertaking group treatment
of any kind in a school. A basic course in group process and/or
dynamics is essential, and may be available through a nearby
college or university. Knowledge of human growth and behavior is
important, including normal and pathological etiology. Basic
understanding of treatment approaches - listening, empathy, study,
diagnosis and treatment - is also important to the group worker, as
is an introductory course in group treatment.

Those of you who are lacking some or all of the above training
might want to begin with task, skill, or educational groups or a
very limited version of the common problem group. One new worker,
for instance, did a nice job of handling an eight-week group of
seniors in high school who needed to think through what they wanted
to do when they graduated. These were healthy kids, with real
problems and concerns, and many strengths on which to build. It was
a good beginning for this worker. Perhaps the most important
quality of a group therapist in a school is a basic committment to
try. If you have first hand knowledge that groups can work, that is
even better. If you have never run a group yourself, do you have a
real interest in finding out how they work with students? Are you
curious about the possibilities for and power of groups? Do you
have the support of the administration? Are you "stacking the
deck" for maximum success? I feel strongly that group treatment
ought to be a rewarding experience for you and your students. The
best way to begin a group is to define an issue that is of interest
to you, find students who are hurting in this area, and compose the
group carefully. If you have a good experience, so will the group
members.

Not all groups in schools are formed groups. There may be
times when a natural friendship group wants to see you about areas
of concern to them. They may come en masse and ask to meet with you
on a regular basis about some specific issue. You might be able to
be very helpful to them, but before you take them on be sure that
you find out their goals for the group. Why do they want to see
you? What do they hope to accomplish? How will the group meeting
be different from the times they are socializing together? Try to
find out their "hidden" agendas. Are they looking for a way to be
together during the school day? Do they want to get out of a
particular class? If the group members have mutual attainable
goals that fit in with some which are of interest to you, it can be
a fun group. Remember that in this situation most of the norms,
roles and decision-making properties are inherited - they come with
the group - and those which might be destructive may be hard to
change. If, however, the group really wants something for

themselves, you have little to lose by trying.

In Summary

The above are just the bare bones of some of the wide variety of ways to lead therapeutic groups in schools. Take a moment now to ponder which of these methods might be interesting to you. What would you like to try? What is possible within your particular school? What is the attitude of most of the teachers toward different types of groups? Are there other personnel with whom you might like to run a group? What is in it for you to begin a group program? Once you have looked at some of these questions, you may be ready to undertake development of groups for therapeutic purposes.

Chapter Twelve

THE SCHOOL AS A SYSTEM - THE FACULTY AS A GROUP

There is a direct relationship between the way a faculty works together as a group and the overall atmosphere of the school. The faculty norms, roles and other components of group functioning are important not only within the faculty group, but between the faculty and the school as a system, and between teachers and students. The school system includes not only faculty, but administrative and supportive staff. Secretarial and custodial personnel are of tremendous importance to a well-functioning school, and must be considered in any discussion of the system. Many times the office secretary has a great deal of power, and it is important to include her in making some of the decisions which she is expected to implement. An irritable janitor can have the entire school on edge, where one who takes pride in the building and relates comfortably to students, can help develop a spirit of comradery in keeping the facilities clean. The principal has a great deal of influence over school operation and spirit. Each administrator makes his own contribution to the school, depending upon his personality, goals and style of work.

Types of Administration

In some schools the administrator or principal is clearly the controlling person, at least openly, and most of the operation of the school revolves around his leadership. It is as if he were the head of a group of followers with teachers and other staff responding to him, agreeably or hostilely, openly or covertly. There are frequently people behind the scenes who have tremendous influence over that type of leader, but the formal or open agreement is that the principal or administrator is clearly in charge and the task of the faculty is to pursue the mandates of that individual. There are a number of things that exist in this form of administration. When one person is in obvious control, you usually know what is expected of you. You know what the demands of the administration are, and the ground rules you must follow to succeed. These are understood by faculty and children alike, with little questioning.

This autocratic type of administration, however, does encourage faculty subgrouping as teachers decide whether or not to support certain decisions. There can be plotting against the principal, and underground actions in an attempt to make possible changes which otherwise might not occur. The "parental" attitude which this method of administration includes may lead to "adolescent acting out" on the part of the faculty. In one such school, faculty were required to stay until exactly 3:45 PM each day. The principal stood and watched the door to see that no one left early. This created some covert acting out against the principal. Because they were not free to discuss their frustration at being treated like children, they began to act in child-like ways. Teachers who ordinarily would remain in their classrooms long after the school day was over, began to leave exactly on time. Also in this school there was a good deal of absenteeism, (what the teachers called "mental health days"), and a fair amount of other passive-aggressive behavior. The other thing that happened in this school was that subgroups of faculty banded together to criticize the way the school was being run without taking any responsibility themselves for making constructive changes.

Though having strong dictator-like leadership is very difficult in many ways, some faculty members prefer this type of administration. They like the clear expectations and are glad that the principal assumes total responsibility for the operation of the school. If an administrator makes all the decisions, he is in control of things that go well, but he is also responsible for everything that goes wrong. In the school I just described, every time something went awry the faculty would blame it on the administrator. As a matter of fact, one winter day I entered the school to find that the heat was off. Several faculty members were standing around complaining that the absent administrator had neglected to get the furnace cleaned before school started, but no one had thought to call the repair company. This form of leadership can be viable or destructive, depending to a large extent on the openness of the administrator to input and on the expectations of the faculty. Are teachers comfortable following the orders of the principal? Do they share the responsibility for the educational goals of the school? Does he include them in the decision-making process even though the final decision is his? Do the teachers feel that their opinions are valued? In this form of leadership open communication is a must, and yet frequently at a premium.

Another type of administration is that in which key faculty run the school and the principal abstains from a leadership position for a variety of reasons. A principal may trust his faculty to be able to manage the school day, and not feel that it is important to participate. He might feel that his prime job is relating to parents and the superintendent, rather than attending to internal school matters. More likely, he is afraid to take on strong faculty who seem to know what they are doing and do not want to be led. He may have been hurt in the past and, therefore, is self-protective. Schools run by faculty without the guidance of administration may run smoothly if the faculty pulls together, but more often suffer from lack of consistent and strong leadership. There may be constant struggles for power among different faculty subgroups, while the principal hides in his office in order to stay out of the middle. Just as a classroom needs a teacher who is also a leader, most faculties need someone to offer direction. If the principal does not assume that role, someone else does. A respected faculty member may take leadership and make major decisions, sometimes allowing the principal to take credit or blame for them. But quite possibly there is an internal struggle for leadership among two or three chief faculty which may never be successfully resolved.

It is probably obvious by now that my professional bias is that the type of administration that works the best is a cooperative management system between principal and faculty, with each sharing some responsibility for the implementation of school goals and everyone being a part of the decision-making process.

An Ideal School

Knowing that it is an impossible one, let me share with you my dream of an ideal school. This dream has evolved over the course of ten years of consulting in different school districts and seeing some schools functioning very well together and others where the conflict and constant crises within the school took so much time and energy that there was not much left over for teaching. My ideal school is a place where everyone's goal is to provide an environment in which growth and learning can take place, and where everyone who enters the door is respected for the contribution which he or she can make toward that goal. It is a school where people feel valued and significant and assume responsibility for helping others feel important. In the same way that I have advocated that teachers work with students in cooperative ways, in this school the principal respects his teachers, expects them to participate in the decision-making process and is free to share with them his mistakes as well as his strengths. There is a mutual agreement that faculty will understand and support his attempts to be a good administrator, the same way they expect him to work with them regarding their strengths and weaknesses as teachers. If something goes amiss in this school, the parties involved meet together to figure out what went wrong and how they can work together to make it right.

The No Fault School. This ideal school operates on what I would call a No Fault basis. The vast majority of schools I have visited are Fault schools. In a Fault school when something goes wrong, the important thing is to find somebody to blame. If there is a problem in the classroom you try to find someone to pin it on. If you cannot find someone to blame, it might mean that there is something wrong with you, that it is your fault. Or, perhaps the incident occurred because the principal did not give you enough support so it is really his fault. This need to find fault which is so prevalent in many schools is the essence of destructiveness when it comes to working cooperatively to provide a safe learning milieu.

In one high school where I was consulting, an incident occurred in which fault finding progressed right down the line. A student made a remark which made the teacher extremely angry and she threw the student out of class. Because she was so angry the teacher immediately sent a "referral" down to the office requesting disciplinary action for that student. After class, the student came to the teacher, apologized for his behavior and asked to be readmitted. Because this was a Fault system the teacher was in a bind. If she readmitted the student and withdrew the referral she would be admitting that she had acted precipituously. Knowing the vice principal of this school she was afraid that he would judge her harshly. On the other hand, she felt the student was genuinely sorry and deserved another chance. Not knowing what else to do, she let the student return to class, and yet feeling very guilty, allowed the referral to stand. The vice principal felt a responsibility to punish the young man in order to support the teacher, even though she felt the teacher was wrong. When I talked with her later about the incident and expressed my concern that the young person had been disciplined <u>after</u> he and the teacher had already resolved the issue, she said, "Well, we have our eye on that teacher and she may not have her contract renewed at the end of the year, but we have to support her in the meantime, even at the expense of the student."

It seems like everybody lost and nobody won. Because the school environment did not permit mistakes, everybody got punished and everything that occurred was blamed on someone else. I wonder what might have happened if that same situation had taken place in a different school with a supportive environment? If the teacher had felt valued, she might not have lost control as quickly as she did over the insolence of the student. But if she had, and if she had sent the referral prematurely, a supportive school system would have permitted her to go to the vice principal and say, "That student really got to me, but I don't think I want to continue with the referral. I'd like to work it out with him myself." That would have ended that administrative involvement and then she could have sat down with the student and talked with him about what had made her so angry. Instead of being punished the student would have had to take responsibility for his own behavior and make plans to change the way he treated the teacher.

There is something about punishment which is positive and negative at the same time. On the one hand, particularly in a junior high school, some children need to have rules to test, to push against. For these situations, providing some form of repercussion may be helpful. On the other hand, punishment lets children "off the hook" and they may feel they do not have to assume responsibility for their behavior as long as they are willing to take the consequences.

I was amused one day when I walked into a junior high school and found a very angry principal walking up and down the hall among 15 children who were sitting on the floor, writing 50 times each, "I will not be tardy again." She said that for every minute they were late they would have to write that sentence ten times. I found some young people outside plotting together about how many times they were willing to write that statement, so that they could be that many minutes late to school. As a matter of fact, one girl came in ten minutes late. She had written, "I will not be tardy again" a hundred times at home so that she would have an extra ten minutes to finish watching a television show before she came to school. For her it was worth it.

You may think that behaving that way is childish and irresponsible, and you may be right. But I wonder how many of us park in an illegal parking place because we are in a hurry and it is worth paying the fine to get the convenience. I am not sure, but I think that kind of response to punishment is natural.

Because the tardiness in the junior high school was getting increasingly out of hand, I suggested to the principal that she inform the children that the punishment system was no longer in effect and they would have to start coming on time. I also suggested she ask each teacher to discuss with her entire class how frustrating it was when the students straggled in, and to ask the students to assume responsibility for seeing that this did not continue to happen. With a great deal of skepticism the principal agreed to try the plan of removing the punishment for children who were late and instead asking them to see that they came on time. Obviously I would not have included this example if it had not worked so well. Within three days, instead of having 15 children tardy, there were two or three with some very legitimate excuses, and peer pressure from class members helped these students get to school on time too. The Fault system of schools, while it is a natural part of many bureaucracies, is not conducive to creating responsibility for behavior.

My ideal No Fault school is one where people share the excitement, planning and responsibility. Students _and_ faculty are free to make mistakes, and the expectation of the group members for one another is that when someone makes a mistake others are to try to help, rather than to sit back and blame. This attitude starts with the administration, and the sharing process of administrators and faculty needs to be two-way. A principal ought to be free to help out faculty who make errors in judgement and at the same time expect staff to assist him if he gets into difficulty.

There are constructive ways to develop this mutual support system within a faculty group. I am frequently asked to work with a faculty at the beginning of the school year to try to develop a No Fault system. Often an outside consultant is very helpful, but I do not believe that it is always essential. Some principals or other administrators can implement this process themselves. The No Fault system starts with the assumption that everybody who comes into the school is entitled to have a good day. Then the question is what are some of the things that can help this come about? One principal asked this question in the first faculty institute day. In small groups the faculty was requested to draw up several sets of goals. One set included broad school goals. Another set of goals were for the faculty - what would make school a good place for them? Another was goals for the students - what is it that we want our students to learn? As the administrator helped the faculty outline these goals, she tried to assure that the four important ingredients (safety, something in it for them, something to give and somebody cares) were all included, not only that day but in the future goal setting. These are just as important and significant for faculty and administration as for children. After she helped the faculty outline some basic goals and they decided what type of environment they wished the school to provide, they moved toward a plan of implementation by posing several questions. "What can we do together to develop these qualities? What role do we want the principal to play? What can each of us do to facilitate the desired outcome. Knowing that it is going to take some time, and knowing that there is much that must be undone, as well as begin, where should we start? As these questions were discussed the faculty developed a commitment to work toward a No Fault approach - a freedom to make mistakes as long as you learn from them - and a general agreement that faculty, staff and students can support one another. This required some reworking of some of the old group norms which were operating in the faculty and prohibited the openness discussed above.

Many faculties have a norm, for example, of "Always be polite, even if you don't mean it," or "Never show a colleague how you really feel." These norms usually develop in a Fault school where much of the complaining and arguing is behind peoples' backs. I can go into a school and in about 30 minutes tell you if it is a Fault or No Fault school. One of my prime diagnostic sources is the faculty lounge. In the faculty lounge I can see if people are listening to one another, showing concern for each other and offering suggestions to teachers with problems, or if it is a place where a great deal of nonproductive complaining and griping goes on with nobody offering any suggestions or attempting to make anything better. In the latter situation if a teacher does something to make another teacher angry, it is rarely dealt with honestly. The offended teacher usually goes to someone else to complain. How the faculty handles disagreements with one another and with the administration is an important criteria of their ability to function cooperatively as a group.

Let me explain what I am not saying. I am not saying that all members of a faculty have to like one another, socialize together or be comrades and confidants to one other. That is neither possible nor desireable. There will always be subgroups of people who like each other better than other people, and who trust each other more than the rest of the faculty; but it is extremely important to see that these natural social friendships do not interfere with an overall atmosphere of mutual acceptance in the school.

The Ladder Concept. Once you feel you can make a mistake and still be valued as a teacher you may want to think about developing the "ladder concept" in your school. The ladder concept gives each person in the school an invisible ladder to carry around which can be used to help your colleagues get down out of a tree if they get caught there. I believe that working with human beings is an extremely emotionally laden endeavor and that it is not possible to be a good teacher without, at some times, having your emotions take over. The times when I temporarily lose control of myself are the times when I would love to have somebody there with a ladder to help me get down out of the tree. That person must be someone who is not caught up in the incident himself, and who cares enough about me to see that I do not get myself further out on the limb than I already am.

A fourth grade teacher was out of control, temporarily, in her fury at a girl in her class. This girl, Sara, had been aggravating, insolent and difficult to work with from the first day of school. The teacher, Mrs. S., had tried everything she could to reach Sara, who seemed to be not only unreachable, but also able to make her feel inadequate. Sara's message was, "I'm not responding because you are not a good teacher," and there was a piece of Mrs. S. which believed that, though the girl was wrong. The last straw was one day when Sara was late from recess and Mrs. S. looked up as she came in and asked her why she was late. Sara's defensive response was, "There was no reason to come to class - nothing interesting ever happens here." The teacher lost control, took Sara out in the hall and started screaming at her. This strong emotional response was a very honest and natural one under the circumstances. How many teachers could have taken this all year without at some point letting it get to them?

A teacher walking by realized that Mrs. S. was temporarily out of control and that she needed a ladder to get down out of her tree before she said or did something she would be sorry about. Because this was a No Fault shcool the teacher who was not upset was able to extricate Mrs. S. from the situation by going up and saying, "It looks like Sara has really gotten to you. Why don't you let me take her off your hands for a while?" This removed Sara from the wrath of Mrs. S. and gave each of them a chance to calm down. The helping teacher, the one with the ladder, then walked off with Sara and without having to punish her or bawl her out was able to calmly comment, "You really made Mrs. S. furious. Is that what you wanted to do?" She then talked for a few minutes with Sara about what her goal was in relation to that teacher. After their talk, Sara came and sat in her classroom for a while until Mrs. S. sent word that she was ready to have the girl return.

How different this approach is from one where a teacher, trying to be supportive by not interfering lets another teacher go on and on until real damage is done; or where a teacher also attacks the child in a false need to protect the angry teacher. The ladder concept is possible only when the faculty agrees that these outbursts are normal and natural, and act as helping agents rather than judges. The ladder concept can also work among students in a classroom. Children can learn to help each other but the tone must be set within the faculty. The guideline is: the person who is in control is the one responsible for helping make the situation better. As the faculty masters this approach, then they can educate their students to do the same thing - to carry ladders to help both students and teachers down out of trees when they begin to do something which could be destructive to themselves or somebody else.

Conflict Management. Even in an ideal school there will, of course, be conflicts. Some of these conflicts occur among subgroups; some of them may be theoretical in nature and others much more practical. Some conflict is healthy for a school and a good exchange of ideas and suggestions contributes greatly. If the conflicts which arise are resolved in a supportive way, or there is consensus (or even agreement not to reach consensus), the school can exist with its conflicts without real difficulty. If, on the other hand, the conflicts are driven underground and acted out rather than talked out there may be real problems with communication in general.   If one conflict cannot be discussed openly, it is difficult for any conflict to be overtly resolved. But, because working in schools is so emotionally laden, it is not unusual for a faculty not to want to have to deal with conflict.   I talked with a teacher who said, "I just can't stand any more hassles.   When two faculty members begin to argue I want to get up and leave."   I can certainly understand how she feels, and yet if a norm develops in that school that it is not acceptable to air differences, then the disagreements will be handled covertly which will create another problem.

One district in which I consult has two high schools, each of which resolved the same conflict in a different way.   The issue was whether or not to have a "smoking room" for students.   Faculty differed greatly on the issue of students smoking in school.   Some felt that smoking was dangerous and to allow it was setting a bad example and extremely destructive for students.   Others felt that some young people were going to smoke anyway and that rather than drive it into the washrooms, they would like to provide a smoking area on the condition that the students agreed (and kept the agreement) to confine all smoking to that one area.   One of the reasons that this was a loaded issue, of course, was because there was conflict among the faculty themselves about whether or not they should smoke in school.   Some teachers complained, "We can't even go into the teachers' lounge because the smoke is so heavy we have trouble breathing!"   Others said, "Smoking is a part of life and we ought to accept it."

In one of the two schools an agreement was reached which was satisfactory to everybody - something that everyone could live with - even though there were parts of the agreement that nobody liked. In the other school, a decision was made based on strong opinions which were expressed by a few loud vocal faculty members, and 3/4's of the faculty did not really agree.   They were hesitant to challenge the other faculty, so gave in rather than fighting for their own beliefs.   If I am pushed into acquiesing to a rule which I really disagree with, the likelihood that I will actively enforce it is not very great.   Even though I know I should, I tend not to. In the school where the faculty really worked together to find something that everybody in the school could live with, the solution that was agreed upon was supported by all of the faculty. In the other school, the solution worked only sporadically.   Some faculty closed their eyes when they found children smoking and others became extremely rigid.   There was no cooperative enforcement of the policy which had been developed in that school.

Now, exploration of the question of permitting smoking in school or anywhere else could easily fill another whole book.   The point here is that the way the decision was made, and the willingness and ability of the faculty to support it, was inalterably intertwined.

The Value of Diversity

This leads to the whole issue of how a school can accept and use differences among faculty to strengthen the program.   One of

the things that is exciting to me about some faculties is their
diversity. I would hate to be in a school where everybody was the
same and where norms were developed which said that we should all
operate in the same mold. In my ideal school each faculty member
would have some strengths and concerns of his own which would be
known to other faculty members and respected by them. Each teacher
would be free to develop his program as he chose, to utilize his
strengths, and to fit within the broad overall curriculum and
school goals. There would be a minimum of expectations for faculty
members to act the same way. Of course master school rules and
state laws are mandates which all teachers have to enforce, but
there are many rules which can differ from class to class. There is
no reason why every classroom should have the same rules, as a
matter of fact there are contraindications for that structure.
Insisting that all teachers follow the same rules inhibits their
freedom to teach in ways which are comfortable to them. Students
know when you are enforcing a rule in which you do not believe, and
it can create mistrust on the part of some of the students. On the
other hand, students are very able to adapt to different rules in
different classrooms. They are not only aware of, but responsive
to, contrasting requirements of teachers.

One seventh grade teacher said, "I know there is nothing wrong
with chewing gum, but there is something about seeing all those
young people with their mouths going all the time that drives me up
a wall. I just can't stand it." Once she felt free enough to have
her own particular bias she was able to say to her students, "It may
not make sense to you, but gum chewing is so annoying to me that
when I see you I can't teach. I think more about your mouths going
than I do about the subject, so in my class you can't chew gum." Of
course, the students' immediate response was, "But Mr. Jones let us
chew gum in his class!"   This teacher, fortunately, felt
comfortable enough with herself, and Mr. Jones, to say, "Marvelous!
I'm delighted that Mr. Jones lets you chew gum in his class. Chew
all the gum you want there, but not here." It is this acceptance of
yourself and your own expectations and desires that frees you in a
No Fault school to set different rules for behavior in your
classroom than there are in others. That is perfectly all right.
What is not okay is for you to try to get all teachers to outlaw gum
chewing because it is offensive to you. That is where schools run
into difficulty. There are certain behaviors which some teachers
expect from their students that others do not, and faculty members
ought to have permission from each other as well as the administration to formulate with their classes their own rules, based on
the needs of the teacher and desires of the students.

A Challenge

Take a step back now and think about your school. What does go
on in your teachers' lounge? What expectations do you have of each
other and your principal? What kind of support system exists? Do
you have a desire to get away from backbiting and work toward mutual
support? Is it possible for disagreements to be aired between the
people that disagreed rather than pushed underground? These are
all important questions and challenges.   Take a look at your
faculty as a group. How do you relate to one another, and how does

the administration relate to you? Or, if you are an administrator,
how fulfilling is your relationship with the faculty? What do you
want to preserve? What would you like different?

Such an analysis may seem like an overwhelming and insurmountable task.   You might begin by asking yourself, if you could
walk into school tomorrow and have <u>one</u> thing different in the way
faculty relates to one another and to the administration, what
would it be?   If you could only have one change, where would you
start? Now that you have that in mind think about whether you can
go to school tomorrow and begin to effect that one change.   If you
start making <u>your</u> day in school better for you, I have no question
that your students will be more excited about coming to your class.

Chapter Thirteen

THE EVER-PRESENT FACULTY COMMITTEE

No book on use of groups in schools can be complete without some discussion about school committees. Few faculty members go through a school year without serving on at least one committee, and in many schools committees are an extremely important influence, positive or negative. One principal said that he thinks that committees are the core around which the rest of the school program revolves. Much of what has been discussed earlier in this book is relevant to this chapter as well, but there are several additional considerations which can be taken into account by one who is trying to improve the committee work of a faculty. As stated throughout the previous chapters, the completion of a task is directly related to the personal and process issues which are present in the groups. As in any group, task completion in committees depends to a large extent on the norms, roles and decision-making qualities of the group.

There are many types of committees. Some are long standing groups with an ongoing purpose, such as pupil personnel teams, curriculum committees and departmental groups. Others are specific task committees which are established and organized to complete a particular job. Still others are formed to develop a solution to some problem within the school. Both of the latter types of committees disband when the task is completed or the problem is solved. Whichever type of committee you are currently a member of, or whatever multitude of committees have your name on the roster, there are group process issues of which you will want to become aware. Despite the power of some of these committees, and the important tasks that they often undertake, their formation is frequently haphazard and without regard to the qualities necessary for positive group functioning.

What Makes Committees Run?

The first consideration in making a committee succeed is selection of a task or purpose which is manageable. If the purpose of a committee is to decide on a plan of action in response to some problem or difficulty, then it must be possible to accomplish that goal in the time allowed, and the committee needs to know that their conclusion will be respected. Sometimes goals are not achieved because they are unattainable as originally stated, and sometimes committee members do not make an investment in goal attainment because they do not believe that their work will be accepted. As one committee chairman said, "There's no reason to put a lot of time and energy into making a plan of action. After we make our report the principal is going to do what she wants anyway." Sometimes restructuring and narrowing goals assists the committee functioning. For example, a committee developed to study and plan ways to handle lunch room chaos is more likely to have its members successfully work together and complete their task than a committee to "discuss discipline". The latter topic is so broad that a committee could discuss it for years, and unless they narrowed their goals, frustrated committee members would have little to show for their efforts. A global purpose is self-defeating, not only because it is impossible to accomplish, but because of the disappointment and resentment which build up in the committee members. This dissatisfaction often leads group members to act out against the administration, against each other, or both.

A second important consideration is the way faculty assignments to committees are made. The most effective committees are those which are formed out of interests of the faculty and their desire to undertake a task. There will be some committees, however, which are necessary but which have lower priority for the faculty members personally, such as a task group to plan some minor program, or a decision-making committee where members have no particular investment in the outcome. If the committee is a "forced" group, with assignments made by administration without trying to find out who is interested in serving, the resistance is often quite obvious, and the first job of such a committee chairman is to help each person get something for themselves from the group experience. One chairman was in charge of a committee to evaluate and come up with ideas for better ways to police the student washrooms, which were messy and smelly much of the time. He found a very resistant group of committee members. Many of them resented the assignment, feeling that it was not their job to study washrooms. Others were simply not interested one way or the other. The chairman felt it was important to do something about the problem and that if the committee did not make suggestions, nothing would be accomplished. He called the next meeting at his home and followed it with a buffet supper. Group members found it more pleasant to discuss the problem in a home, and since they had a chance to socialize later, they quickly got into the task and came up with some good suggestions which were implementable.

There are other instances where members themselves can make an unpleasant task into a pleasant group experience. Some groups can complete unsatisfying jobs expediently and competently because they enjoy each other as people and the social aspects make the unfulfilling aspects bearable. Some group members seem to have a knack for making the most menial jobs fun to do. One resentful group of teachers were asked to stay after school to complete year end curriculum reports. The mood was lightened when one of the members developed ways to make a game out of the writing, and the group members had a grand time together as they completed the task.

Not all committees work out that well. In a school where I taught, we were assigned to a committee to discuss grades. The administration was concerned that our grading was not uniform from teacher to teacher and that some of us were "too easy" and others "too hard". Each faculty member was comfortable with the way he or she used grades, and was somewhat antagonistic toward the administration for interfering with that process. Also, some teachers were afraid that if their grading pattern became known to the other teachers, they would be subject to criticism. Still others were afraid to discuss grading because they did not want to offend their colleagues. Because of these, and other more subtle reasons no one volunteered to serve on the "grade committee". A desperate administrator finally appointed a committee and said a report was due before the next faculty meeting. The committee dutifully met, discussed the members' dissatisfaction with the grading system, kidded around about the school, but had no particular interest in getting down to work. Finally one of the members said, "We have to make a report! What are we going to say?" Someone suggested that we recommend that grades be eliminated altogether. While no one particularly liked this idea, it was adopted unanimously so that the committee members would not have to grapple with the grade issue, and yet still complete their assignment. When the report was made at the faculty meeting it was strongly attacked and the committee members responded, "Okay, you do it." To this day the issue of grading has not been resolved.

Still another important consideration is the role of the committee chairman. Even when the task is clear and manageable, and the committee members have some investment in the outcome, they may have difficulty getting the job done. Some groups have trouble accepting the leadership, or chairmanship, of a peer. Or, if the committee is chaired by an administrator, the general feelings about that person carry over to group functioning. Sometimes a principal decides to be a committee member and appoints another chairman. Occasionally this works, but usually it is clear that the principal is there pretending to be a peer, and that she really has the final say. Therefore, most of the suggestions of committee members are made with an eye on the principal to catch her reaction, rather than to each other, or to the assigned chairman. My own experience as an administrator has proved that it is extremely difficult to try to be "one of the gang". I can be very much a part of what is going on but not a true peer. There are some administrators who feel that they can be a peer at certain times, and not at others, and some faculties which seem able to accept this role change, but usually it does not work well and leads to angry disappointment. If an administrator who is trying to be a peer refuses to give his opinions, and the faculty or staff do not feel free to respond until they know what his thoughts are, the group may reach a frustrating impasse. Some schools like it best when the administrator either chairs the committee, or lets the group do their job and report back.

There is still another factor which affects the cooperative working together of a committee. Often outside pressures upon committee members cause conflict and difficulty in problem resolu- tion. A teachers' association negotiating committee was meeting to decide the first round of terms for their new contract talks. Members were just beginning to work well together in this huge effort, when each found himself bombarded with suggestions and comments from teachers who were not on the committee. This input was helpful, but made resolution more difficult since the expecta- tions were continuously changing. As one member put it, "I feel caught in a vice between my own beliefs, the values of the other committee members, and the constant advice and pushing from outsiders."

What happened in this committee is representative of what happens in all groups. The forces of content, process and personal extend beyond the group itself once again to the broader environment within which the group resides. Just as in a classroom, there are not only internal pressures at each of the three levels, but external pressures as well. This is true for most of us in all of our jobs within a school, but somehow with committees, perhaps because we are working with our peers toward cooperative efforts, these pressures are even harder to handle.

A Positive Committee Structure

If all of these factors complicate the group process, how can you set up an efficient committee structure within a school? My first suggestion is to cut down on the number of committees. Committees are like weeds - they tend to grow and grow and the greater the number of committees the more they tend to get in the way of school operation. One school which did a review of their committee structure found three different committees working on the same task, with the work of one negating the work of another. It is not unusual within a given school to have more committees than there are faculty members, and one school which I recently visited even had a "Committee on Committees". Recognizing that in a democratically run school committees are important, begin to set priorities for your school. What issues need to be handled by committee? Which are best decided administratively? Which can be resolved by each teacher alone? Are there several committees doing jobs that one committee could do? One junior high school faculty found several different groups each of which was planning some upcoming social event. When one member complained, "As soon as I get finished with one event, I'm drafted to help plan another," the faculty decided to start the next year with an ongoing "person committee" which had responsibility for planning the social calendar for the year, reaching out to people who were sick, and generally looking out for the well-being of each member of the faculty. This committee developed a cohesive spirit during the year, and their interest in each other spread to the rest of the school. The task of looking out for one another was completed much more efficiently than it had been when several different committees tried to do similar jobs.

In your school are there committees that are no longer needed? Perhaps they have outlived their original purpose or have accomplished nothing in the past few months. Maybe there are committees which might be combined to reduce the replication of discussion. If there are time limited committees, how quickly can they complete their task? Which committees in your school should be ongoing and which short term? Ongoing committees play an important role in schools if the members work well together and have a reason to continue to meet. Many task groups, however, work best on a time limited basis. Task groups which have focused, attainable, narrow goals and a limited life span seem to be more successful than those which drag on and on.

After your review of the current committee structure in your
school, look at the tasks which need to be done which can be
accomplished by committee.   There may be ongoing departmental
business which requires active group participation, or a pupil
personnel team's continuous relating to each other around problem
children, or an ongoing committee to work consistently toward
improving the school milieu. What are the major categories of work
that can best be done in committees and which of these can be
accomplished in a short period of time? The faculty can help design
a committee structure which makes sense for your particular school
and provides opportunities for active participation of teachers in
areas of special interest to them. You may also find district-wide
committees in which some of your faculty will want to participate.

If you want to support committee functioning within schools,
membership in such groups should be considered part of the regular
job load, and acknowledged as that.   In one school, participation
on committees was poor and the principal complained to me that the
faculty did not seem interested in serving on some of these
important task groups.   When I asked the teachers about his
concern, one responded, "Being on a committee doesn't count in this
school. Last year I was on seven different committees and worked
like mad as the chairman of one, but when my evaluation came around
it was never mentioned." Other faculty felt that committee membership was just one more thing added to an already full schedule.
Administrators who want to have well-functioning committees should
see them as part of the regular job of each teacher and must allow
both time and recognition for committee work.

Another important factor is assisting committees to do their
jobs is the way they are composed. Do your committees consist of
people who wish to serve? Are they representative of the school
population? Are the basic maintenance roles accounted for? Was
the chairman selected by the committee members? You will think of
many other basic composition issues which are important to task
group work.

Bailing Out a Sinking Committee

As with all groups, the best way to insure successful task
completion is to form the committee in ways which support task
accomplishment. There will, however, on occasion be some committee
which seems to be floundering. You may be the chairman or a member
when this begins to happen, and whatever role you are playing you
can be of assistance if you choose to. If you are the chairman and
see your task group begin to drown, the best approach is to point
out what is happening and ask the committee to help. Some of the
problem solving approaches discussed in Chapter 4 will be of
assistance. If you are a group member and the chairman is not
acting in a helpful manner, then you must decide whether to fight,
pull back and watch or take a more constructive form of action.
Your decision will be based upon your investment in the group, your
own hidden and open agendas, your current priorities, and your
style of working with groups. A member of a pupil personnel team
saw the discussion of one "problem" child greatly influenced by
competition between last year's teacher and this year's teacher.

It seemed that the boy's former teacher, Mr. B., was afraid that if the student made a successful adjustment this year it was a negative commentary on his teaching since the boy had had trouble in his class. This message was subtly being sent by the current teacher and some of the other staff in the meeting. The defensiveness of Mr. B. kept him from sharing openly some of the difficulties the boy had experienced last year, which was important to formulating a plan for this period.

A social worker at the meeting noticed the conflict and after thinking about the best way to intervene pointed out that both teachers obviously cared a great deal about this boy, and that each had strengths which were used in trying to help the boy adjust to the classroom. She said that the groundwork laid by Mr. B. could now be used to support the boy's experience this year. This warm, supportive statement brought the two teachers together in their work - neither needed to prove to the other that they were competent. Mr. B. began to relax and acknowledge that there had been things he had done which might be worth considering, and the current teacher was able to listen to his suggestions.

There are many other ways that this group member could have been helpful, but the social worker who assisted the process selected an intervention at the personal level which made sense to her. When we discussed it after the meeting she said, "I was just a member of the group and didn't feel free to challenge what was happening at the process level, but I could not see that anyone would mind my giving support. There is too little support given around here." How I wish more persons within a school operated in that manner.

Putting what is happening "on the table" might also have been helpful in such a situation. Without judging, it is possible to comment that "we seem to be having trouble agreeing, I wonder why?" One chairman asked committee members who were locked in conflict what they thought was in it for them not to reach resolution. This forced the group to either solve the issue, or look at reasons why they did not. Here, too, it is extremely important not to judge, but to ask questions which require answers which will help group members see for themselves what is holding them up.

There is an old, useful saying that "If you are not part of the solution, you are part of the problem." I agree with this to a large extent, though I also feel that in a school which makes tremendous demands upon everyone who sets foot in the door, you must set priorities about where to place your energy. I have consciously sat back and watched the process when I might have been able to help, just because I had no more energy to devote to problem solving at that time. Other times I have been a real fighter to get my point across. I am most effective when I am able to understand the group process, point it out, and then give the group the responsibility of making their own desired changes. Whichever you choose to do, as a committee member or chairman, understanding what is happening in the group will be helpful.

Chapter Fourteen

OUTSIDE GROUPS THAT AFFECT SCHOOL FUNCTIONING

As discussed in Chapter 1, there are many outside groups that seriously affect the functioning of a school. Some of these groups are very supportive to the school, the teachers and the children. Others appear to be in opposition to the mission of the school. Most are somewhere in the middle. Whichever may be the case, each outside group has its own group dynamics and processes which affect the way it relates to the school. In addition, a relationship develops between the outside group as a system and the school as a system which creates a positive, negative or neutral working arrangement. The administrator who is in touch with his school system, and who attempts to understand the working of the varying outside groups which relate to the school can often discover compatible goals which will lead to successful merging of the organization's efforts.

Mutual Goals

Just as goals of groups within a school must be compatible to function in a positive way, goals of the school and the outside organizations with which it comes in contact must be able to live together in order to avoid needless conflict. The principal who acknowledges that each outside group has its own unique goals, who tries to accept these goals, and who finds a way to merge them with school goals has a much better chance of avoiding conflict than the administrator who refuses to acknowledge the goals of other organizations.

In addition, the principal who is able to use the goals of outside organizations, not as impediments, but as stepping stones toward attainment of school goals, may find that groups which have the potential to be adversaries, can instead become allies. In one district, a religious group strongly objected to the use of "explicit" content in the high school family life education course. That community group felt that such education should take place in church and at home, not at school. The principal understood their point of view, though he did not agree with their suggestions. He met with spokesmen from the group to find out what was most important to them, and found ways to make some of the educational goals of the family life curriculum compatible with those of the religious group. He also invited a leader of that outside group to teach one session of the class on the role of religion in the family. This acceptance of the outside group's stance, without backing off of his, led to a cooperative effort on the part of both groups.

Since family life education is frequently a topic around which community groups can rally, one principal tried a different approach. Prior to beginning the program, she established an advisory group of community representatives to review the material, discuss it and make suggestions and comments on it. After the program began, she referred questions and criticisms, as well as accolades, to this school-community group. By letting this committee participate in the process, the finished product was partly theirs, and they were receptive to its implementation. Those parents who became upset or antagonistic to the program were effectively handled by advisory group members.

There are many other community groups which can be utilized effectively to help support schools. Local businesses frequently donate foods, craft materials and other goods and services in exchange for recognition in a school newsletter. Often parents of students in the school work in a business which can be of assistance. One grocer supplied all the ingredients for a monthly "hot dog day" in an elementary school. In exchange, the sixth grade class sent three students every Saturday to help around the store. This joint endeavor led to good relationships between the store and the school; the youths felt proud of their contribution; and everyone in the school benefited in some way.

Often a merging of services can come about by joining the forces with a recreation agency, church or leisure-time group. Providing space in the school for evening meetings of adult groups often leads to closeness with the school, positive regard and willingness to cooperate with community-school events. Take a moment to think about your local community groups. Which are cooperating fully with you? Are there some which are causing difficulty? If so, have you thought about their goals and the possibility of respecting them without infringing upon your aspirations? Are there organizations in your community which might potentially be useful to the school but with which there is no real contact? One high school social studies class did a survey of community groups and found several ways that local groups could be involved in a supportive way with the school. It proved to be a meaningful learning task for the students with excellent side benefits for the school.

Parents' Groups

Parents' groups, as discussed in Chapter 1, are many and varied. But regardless of their composition or purpose, they can influence the functioning and freedom of the school. Some have an inhibiting effect and some a supportive one. Others are rather passive and have little effect on the school at all. There is as wide a variation of types of parents' groups as there are people in them.

Parent-Teacher Associations are formalized parents' groups which relate officially to schools. These groups may be run by both parents and teachers but most of them are operated by parents and have meetings which may be attended by teachers (often at the strong suggestion of the administration). Some PTA's are primarily social clubs and their monthly meetings have programs unrelated to school business. One that I attended recently had a session on flower arranging, and another had a discussion of the latest best selling book. Other Parent-Teacher Associations operate as

auxiliaries to schools. If a school needs something, they try to
get it. One school which lacked sufficient funds for a science trip
asked the PTA to help and members had a bake sale to raise the
needed money. Other PTA's see themselves as watchdogs. The
organization tries to understand the operation of the school and
does not hesitate to criticize when something appears to be
contrary to their views of good education. Most PTA's combine
these functions and it may be difficult to know the origin of a
specific concern. It is essential that a principal work toward
development of compatible goals of the PTA and the school. The
goals do not need to be the same, but should be able to live
comfortably together.

Group goals also have tremendous impact on the ability of the
group members to function cooperatively together. Individual goals
may conflict with one another, and it is then difficult to agree on
broader group purposes. There will be process issues which also
affect the operation of any parents' group and thereby have impact
upon the school. Think of parent organizations connected with your
school. How do they function together as a group? How are officers
selected? Is there an "in" group that really makes all of the
decisions, with other people on the fringe? Are the members free to
express their opinions? How is the agenda decided? These are all
issues which affect not only group operation, but also the
influence of the group upon the school.

In addition, there are less formal types of parents' groups
with which a teacher or administrator may come in contact. Some of
them are action groups. A group of parents may get together to work
toward a change which they feel is important, and which may or may
not be in the best interests of the school. One such group put a
good deal of time and effort into attempts to have the principal
replaced. They felt that she was not sympathetic to the needs of
the local community and wanted a principal who was from the same
ethnic background as the majority of the pupils. Another group
fought hard to obtain additional classrooms because of a serious
space problem. Still another parents' group organized to try to
prevent the closing of a school which had been slated to be shut
down at the end of the school year because of dwindling enrollment.
This last example reflects one of the problems of conflicting
goals. The district wanted to provide good education for the
children at minimum cost. The parents were legitimately concerned
about their property values and the additional time and hassle of
bussing their children to a more distant school. They did not,
however, seem to consider the negative effect on their own children
of continuing in that school and combining three or four grades
into one class because there would not be enough students of the
same age to fill a class. In some district, similar issues are
resolved for politically expedient reasons rather than based on the
educational needs of the children.

Any of these "pressure groups" can be a thorn in the side of an
administrator or teacher. On the other hand, it may be possible for
the administrator who attempts to empathize with their goals to
find some common interest on which both group and school can agree.

These pressure groups of parents have the potential to be viable allies or strong opponents.

In addition to responding to existing groups there are times when schools may want to <u>form</u> groups of parents and other interested community representatives. One principal found himself on the firing line because he had made a number of unpopular arbitrary decisions. After meeting with an outside consultant, he decided to form a principal's advisory group of parents and teachers with whom he discussed basic decisions before they were made. Then, if there were any strong complaints from other parents, he referred them to the parents in the advisory group who seemed very able to handle the criticisms objectively and helpfully. This action got the principal out of the middle without taking away any of his power and freed him to spend more of his time and energy on other school matters.

One kindergarten class found that the children were having difficulty adjusting to school during the beginning of the year. Part of the problem was due to the overprotective attitude of some of the mothers. The teacher decided to have parents' meetings, during kindergarten time, to explain some of the things she was doing in class and enlist their cooperation. Once each week, she turned the class over to an aide who read to the children while she met for half an hour with the parents. As the teacher began to respond to some of the questions raised by the mothers, their anxiety lessened, and the children adjusted better to school. She also discovered that parents who had older children were supportive and helpful to the parents for whom this was a first child in school. While the formal meetings lasted only a few weeks, the relationships which she had established with the parents continued throughout the school year.

Many schools also find it advantageous to establish therapeutic groups for parents of children who are having difficulty in school. If a child is in a special classroom, being in a group of parents whose children are having similar problems is often very reassuring. It is difficult to adjust to the fact that there is "something wrong" with your child (even if that child has the euphemistic label "exceptional"). It is often helpful for a psychologist or social worker to meet with such a group of parents so that the parents will find out that they are not alone. These groups can also give special assistance to parents by teaching techniques for control of behavior, by accepting and understanding feelings, and by discussing some of the marital issues which are bound to arise. In addition, groups can be helpful to parents of normal children who are under situational stress and who are evidencing symptoms – behavioral or affective. These groups have a great deal of impact upon parents, and it is important that they be run by personnel who are trained in the group treatment process. They should be composed with all of the care you would take with any of the therapeutic groups which are discussed in Chapter 11, and attempts to group by common problems and heterogeneous symptoms is just as important in these groups as in groups of children.

The Powers That Be

Every school is part of a district which has its own administration. Each district administration is to some degree governed
by a Board of Education which is ultimately accountable to the
community. The power of each of these groups is affected by the
other groups and is seriously influenced by forces outside the
community. The state funding for education, allocation of monies,
political issues and communication media all have serious impact
upon a school district. The concept of compatible goals holds true
here, too, but it may be much harder to discover what goals are held
by whom than it would be in a less complex network. The last time I
went to a Board of Education meeting, I was impressed by the quality
of leadership represented among the members. Every person there
appeared to have a genuine concern for children as well as concern
for the image of the school distirct within the wider community.
Each Board member also had his or her own personal agenda which made
serving on the board worthwhile to him. Most of these agendas were
compatible with the goals of the board, but it was important for the
superintendent and the board president to know what these personal
agendas were to insure that they did not get in the way of the
decision-making process.

One Board member was an insurance salesman who hoped to locate
prospects as a part of his participation. A woman member was new to
the community and had agreed to run for election as a means to meet
people and become known. Another member was asked to run by his
company as a way of maintaining status in the community where the
company was located. Still another had been coerced to run by a
community pressure group who felt under represented and wanted to
be heard. One member badly needed to feel important and
significant and hoped to use his service on the Board as a means to
gain recognition. Each of these reasons is legitimate and
acceptable. What is important is that instead of judging these
"hidden agendas" they were accepted as viable and respected within
the context of healthy Board functioning.

It was interesting to see how this diverse population of
people fit together. At first, it was amazing that any decisions
were reached because of the varied opinions, goals and backgrounds.
But, each member was accepted as important to the Board by the
president and the superintendent. As the members found their
opinions listened to and considered significant, they all began to
respect and listen to one another. Because the superintendent was
knowledgeable about group process, he took time in meetings for the
group to learn how to relate constructively, establish basic
maintenance roles and develop positive norms.

It is not only a Board of Education that must learn to work
together - each district has an administrative group that functions
together and influences each school within the district. The
necessity for this administrative group to learn to work
supportively together is no less than for teachers to provide a
support system for their students, or a principal to provide a safe
environment for his teachers.

In one small district, a superintendent, assistant superintendent, business manager and pupil personnel director formed the core administrative group which met regularly with the school principals. They enjoyed meeting together, felt free to disagree with one another, got excited about new programs together and found a unified interest in providing good education for the children and a supportive system in the district. The enthusiasm of this administrative group was contagious and as principals went back to their schools feeling happy and valued, this was transmitted to their teachers, who, in turn, carried it into their classrooms. The responsiveness to one another spread throughout the district and teachers knew that they were respected by the administration. This led to increased comfort in working together and an openness which is rarely seen in schools.

Another district, however, had a superintendent who feared for her job. Due to political changes in the city administration this superintendent was afraid to do anything which might "rock the boat". Through the assistant superintendents, she rigidly handed down dictums which she thought would please the city managers and made most of her decisions arbitrarily. When challenged by her staff, she responded, "If you don't like it you can leave." As more and more of the faculty became critical of her approach, she felt herself being backed into a corner, and her responses became attacking and punitive. Her assistants agreed with her to her face, but sabotaged her plans behind her back. They justified their actions because of her dictatorial stance. The situation came to a head when several key teachers requested transfers out of the district and rather than lose them, the Board decided to replace the superintendent. Now, certainly the superintendent handled things badly. There is no doubt, however, that her assistants and other staff did little to help her make it through the storm. They complained, undermined her and waited for her to drown, which she eventually did. If any of the district administrative personnel had known about group process and had had an investment in forming a more supportive group, the crisis need never have come about.

An interesting side effect of the unfortunate situation mentioned above was the carry-over to the next administration. It was not only the first superintendent who suffered, but her negative dictatorial approach was hard to undo. The incoming superintendent found a faculty which was suspicious, avoided responsibility and were awaiting failure. She is now having an extremely difficult time breaking the old patterns of relating and establishing new, more constructive management.

It is the responsibility of the district administrative group to function at a level which will provide for positive decision-making, appropriate avenues for resolution of conflict, and norms which support the educational goals of the district. If they are not operating in a constructive way, the ramifications will be far-reaching. How does the administrative group in your district operate? Do the members support one another? What circumstances support the district educational goals? Which get in the way? What is being done about it?

     In one district, the administration was concerned about the
way the principals of the elementary schools were relating. They
were highly competitive, possessive of information about their
schools and hesitant to cooperate with one another. At the
administrator's request, I met with each principal individually to
discuss their impression of the difficulties. I was not surprised
to discover that every principal was also concerned about these
competitive relationships and was willing to make an effort to work
toward a more supportive system. Following the suggestion of one
of the principals, they went away for a two day retreat to try to
find ways to work more cooperatively. With an outside consultant,
they spent over 20 hours together discussing each person's
individual goals and trying to merge them with district goals.
These discussions, plus the opportunity to have time to enjoy being
together, led to development of a plan for new ways of operating
which supported each individual in his work as well as provided
leadership for the district. They decided to continue to meet
together on a regular basis to share concerns, problem solve and
plan district programs. Obviously, this did not resolve all of
their problems. No one set of meetings can change an entire
district. But the principals gained renewed hope in their ability
to work together and began to form trust relationships. As that
group became strong, they were able to have district-wide impact
upon the administration. How long this will continue and how
important the impact will be on the district is yet to be seen, but
the strides each principal made will stay with him long after this
situation has past.

     The school as a system is greatly influenced by groups - both
inside and outside the school. These groups have tremendous power
over the way a school operates; over the development of a
supportive milieu; and over the attainment of educational goals.
Each of you reading this book also has power in the groups of which
you are a part. How you choose to use, or abuse, that power is up
to you. Knowing what happens in groups, you have the ability to use
your power in very constructive ways. I earnestly believe that you
are entitled to a better day. Do you? Are you willing to work for
it?

A NOTE FROM THE AUTHOR

In this book I have attempted to give the reader some insight into the development and functioning of groups within a school and between schools and the wider community. I have tried to build on this understanding by citing specific examples of possible interventions taken from my many years experience as a teacher and consultant in schools.

How useful this book will be to you as a professional who works within a school depends a great deal upon you. Your interest in the content, your flexibility, your freedom to try new things, and your personal desire to operate in different ways will all influence your use of this material. The degree of trust among the faculty in your school and your relationship with the administration may also have impact upon your ability to use some of the suggestions contained herein. Whatever you decide to try, and wherever you plan to start, it is my hope that this information will prove of some usefulness in your efforts.

Now, I would like to request a favor of you. After you have read this book, digested some of the ideas and made a start in trying something new, will you please drop me a note and let me know your thoughts about the book? I would be particularly interested in any of the suggestions which you feel are especially helpful, or irrelevant, and any sections of the book which you think need revision or expansion. Any comments you care to make will be carefully reviewed, acknowledged and used in possible revisions. You may also use this opportunity to ask any questions which may have risen out of reading this book, or trying some of the suggestions. Within the limits of reality, I shall try to answer as many letters as possible. Your assistance in reviewing this book for readability and utility will be very helpful.

Thank You,

Joy Johnson
7733 Janes Avenue
Woodridge, IL 60515

REFERENCES

Berkovitz, Irving H., (ed.). When Schools Care: Creative Use of Groups in Secondary Schools. New York: Brunner/Mazel Publishers, 1975.

An excellent compilation of articles demonstrating a variety of ways groups can be used in high schools.

Berne, Eric., M.D. Games People Play. New York: Grove Press, Inc., 1964.

A general treatise on the psychology of human relationships including the function of game playing, types of games and how to move beyond them.

Brown, George Issac. Human Teaching for Human Learning: An Introduction to Confluent Education. New York: The Viking Press, 1971.

Specific theoretical and practical examples of ways of combining cognitive and affective learning in classrooms.

Cantwell, Zita M. and Pergrouhi N. Svajian, (ed.). Adolescence: Studies in Development. Itasca, Illinois: F. E. Peacock Publishers, Inc., 1974.

Interesting series of articles linking development of adolescent identity, moral identity, language, abilities and motivation.

Curwin, Richard L. and Barbara Schneider Fuhrmann. Discovering Your Teaching Self: Humanistic Approach to Effective Teaching. Englewood Cliffs, New Jersey: Prentice-Hall, Inc., 1975.

Many concrete suggestions which can help a teacher explore effectiveness of teaching and new approaches to try.

Dreikurs, Rudolf and Pearl Cassel. Discipline Without Tears: What To Do With Children Who Misbehave. New York: Hawthorn Books, Inc., 1972.

Adlerian approach to understanding and controlling the behavior of children in a classroom. Many specific techniques and examples are included.

Glasser, William, M.D. Schools Without Failure. New York: Harper and Row, Publishers, 1969.

Explanations of the ways schools tend to encourage failure in some students. Formulation of ways to help children accept more responsibility for their learning.

Greenburg, Herbert M., _Teaching With Feeling_. New York: The Pegasus Press - a division of The Bobbs-Merrill Company, Inc., 1969.

> After giving a teachers "permission" to be who they are and how they feel, this book helps teachers learn to use their feelings in constructive ways.

Holmes, Monica, Ph.D., Douglas Holmes, Ph.D., and Judith Field, M.A. _The Therapeutic Classroom_. New York: Jason Aronson, Inc., 1974.

> Describes development of therapeutic approaches for use with adolescents who have school problems. Utilization of a mental health team within the classroom is advocated.

Johnson, Joy. _Counseling and Psychotherapy With Adolescents_. A series of six cassette audio tapes available from Instructional Dynamics, 450 E. Ohio, Chicago, Illinois, 60611.

> An in-depth look at the treatment of adolescents and impact on counselor or therapist. Contains specific techniques for intervening in a wide variety of situations.

Johnson, Joy. "School Social Work - A Triangle of Strength". _The Journal of School Social Work_. Vol. 1, No. 1. New Jersey: May 1974.

> A description of the three major ways a social worker should relate to schools - to the system, to other school personnel and to students.

Long, Nicholas J., William C. Morse, and Ruth G. Newman, (ed.). _Conflict in the Classroom: The Education of Emotionally Disturbed Children_. California: Wadsworth Publishing Company, Inc., 1965.

> An excellent fictional and factual synopsis of what happens to disturbed children in school. Includes many helpful ideas for helping these children and the school adjust to each other.

MacLennan, Beryce W. and Naomi Felsenfeld. _Group Counseling and Psychotherapy with Adolescents_. New York: Columbia University Press, 1968.

> A readable, rather simplistic book showing how group counseling can be used in high schools with adolescents.

Mahler, Clarence A. _Group Counseling in the Schools_. Boston: Houghton Mifflin Company, 1969.

> Helps counselors in schools establish and run counseling groups. Includes step-by-step process.

Northen, Helen. Social Work With Groups. New York: Columbia University Press, 1969.

A general description of use of groups in social work practice. Includes dynamics and possible interventions at each stage of group development.

Patterson, C.H. Humanistic Education. Englewood Cliffs, New Jersey: Prentice-Hall, Inc., 1973.

A systematic approach to the development of humanistic education.

Postman, Neil and Charles Weingartner. Teaching as a Subversive Activity. New York: Dell Publishing Company, Inc., 1969.

"An assault on outdated teaching methods." Provocative, entertaining description of what is wrong with today's schools and what can be done about it.

Schrank, Jeffrey. Teaching Human Beings: 101 Subversive Activities for the Classroom. Boston: Beacon Press, 1972.

Specific ideas for teaching touchy subjects to adolescents. Many examples which are fun to read and easily understood.

Simon, Sidney B., Leland W. Howe, and Howard Kirchenbaum. Values Clarification: A Handbook of Practical Strategies for Teachers and Students. New York: Hart Publishing Company, Inc., 1972.

Specific, practical suggestions for activities which involve children in the exploration of their own values.

Yalom, Irvin D. The Theory and Practice of Group Psychotherapy. New York: Basic Books, Inc., Publishers, 1970.

An unusually good exploration of group treatment methods.

TOPICAL INDEX